# EDDIE REESE

## Coaching Swimming, Teaching Life

*I wouldn't say it if I didn't mean it. He's a master of his craft.* **He works his sport better than anybody I've ever seen. He understands it. He gets it. He understands how it all comes together — mind and body. And he understands competition, what second is, and what it takes to be first.**

—RICK BARNES, Head Coach,
University of Tennessee Basketball (ranked #1 in NCAA, 2019)

*When I opened the pre-publication draft, I thought I would get a biography (and there is a bit) or an elite coaching manual (and there is a bit). What I got was a love story. Eddie's love for Elinor and Elinor's reciprocated love, multiplied exponentially.*

*The love affair of Eddie with his swimmers and his swimmers multiplying that into each other, Kris, Elinor and Eddie. There was the surprising love that the entire UT Athletic Department has for Eddie and how he reciprocated that love by coaching a football coach! Then we see the love Eddie has for our sport and how our sport loves him back.*

*Chuck Warner's great lesson to the readers of this book is that love isn't a zero sum game. In every way that Eddie Reese approached his life with love, it went out into the world, multiplied many times over, came back to him much stronger than he sent it out, then spilled out again into the world.*

**Chuck Warner and Dana Abbott tell a master love story. Eddie Reese demonstrates to all of us that when you fill your life with love, you change forever those whom that love touches.** *In turn, you are forever enriched by the return of that love from the world.*

—GEORGE BLOCK, President,
World Swimming Coaches Association

*I always had a great amount of respect and fondness for Eddie while coaching at different programs, and it has only grown since my time here at Texas. Working in close proximity to him these past seven years, I have come to appreciate his insight, his care for people, and how he's remained at the pinnacle of our sport for decades while keeping things in perspective. **I am humbled, inspired, and grateful to share the deck with him.***

—CAROL CAPITANI, Head Coach
The University of Texas Women's Swimming & Diving

*Coach Eddie Reese is a legend in the coaching world and an icon at The University of Texas. He became a great friend to me during our time together at UT and he represents the best of what it means to be a coach and mentor. **The lessons recounted in this book are invaluable for anyone interested in becoming a better leader.***

—COACH MACK BROWN,
Head Coach, University of North Carolina Football –
2005 National Champions-The University of Texas

***There are few times in a life when one is humbled by an exhibition of life and of its depiction. This is one. This book is a must read, not simply for those in the aquatic world, but for every human being searching for a compass in life and a value system that breeds irrefutable respect and unparalleled success. This is the living example.*** *While this story is powerful and inspiring, its presentation is equally so. Chuck Warner is the preeminent author in the world of swimming and masterfully intertwines the extraordinary success of Coach Reese with the powerful virtues that laid the groundwork for that success. And for those outside of the aquatic world, the simple chapter on Eddie's wife, Elinor, would be enough to redirect anyone to a true life of purpose, service, and selflessness. Thank you to Eddie Reese for the example of humanity and of coaching, and to Chuck Warner for bringing to life and light such profound life examples* *and lessons, which seem less and less common in today's society.*

—DON HEIDARY, Board President,
The American Swimming Coaches Association
Co-Head Coach/Founder, Orinda Aquatics

*Eddie Reese took a chance on me as a skinny kid that had been swimming less than a year and helped me become a champion in every sense of the word. Fortunately, we have* **this book that exemplifies what an amazing man Eddie is and how many lives he has impacted.** *I am so incredibly grateful for his mentorship and friendship.*

—ROWDY GAINES, Olympic Broadcaster NBC,
3-Time Olympic Gold Medalist

*I have read hundreds of books on coaching swimming. One, in particular, taught me the importance of laminar flow (I didn't understand it then and I don't understand it now. Nor did it change my coaching career or my life). This book, however, has challenged me to achieve excellence in my coaching both in the pool and with my swimmer relationships. And, although it is not a "self-help book", it provides a blueprint for living a life of impeccable character, being a leader and a role model, and for being a devoted and faithful companion.*

*We often give our swimmers a visual scale of where they are and where they could be. Where they are is at sea level; where they could be is the top of Mt. Everest.* **If I were to use that scale in terms of value for swimming books in general, this book sits at the top of Mt. Everest. I would make it required reading for every coach, in any sport.** *Young coaches would, at the minimum, have a clear sense of what it takes to achieve greatness and how do it with impeccable character.*

—RON HEIDARY, Co-Head Coach/Founder, Orinda Aquatics
Head Coach, Campolindo High School

*Coach Eddie Reese is one of the giants in the history of our sport. His record of achievement in swimming, while remarkable, pales in comparison with his impact on his athletes, their future lives, and the future lives of hundreds of coaches whom he has influenced. That influence comes delivered with humor, warmth, insight and compassion. He is not only one of the "best" coaches ever, he is among the most beloved. Eddie is truly a Legend. America's great coaches comment continuously how much the friendship of Eddie Reese has meant to them.*

*The author, Chuck Warner, himself an accomplished national coach, is also on the way to legend status in writing about swimming. Chuck has been a major force in the American Swimming Coaches Association for decades and a highly sought speaker and panel moderator for clinics for just as long. Chuck is at his best when writing, because he writes about what he loves. And he, like so many other coaches, loves Eddie Reese and loves Coach Reese's impact on our sport.*

***This is a brilliant read…insightful, warm, funny and filled with meaning…just like Coach Reese himself.***

—John Leonard, Executive Director,
The American Swimming Coaches Association

*Chuck Warner takes time to convey the scope of the lives that Eddie has touched, and does it in a way that has me pleasantly reminiscent. But just as important are those around Eddie, near and dear to him, and **there is plenty new [in this book] for even his swimmers to learn, that would light one of our most important mentors up even more.***

—Aaron Peirsol, 5-Time Olympic Champion,
eight years trained under Coach Reese

*"Hey Governor, you're what we call a bankwalker"* was the first indelible conversation I recall with Eddie Reese. Looking down from the edge of the Jamail Swim Center pool, sporting an impish smile, the renowned coach went on to explain that my swimming form was so awful that I obviously grew up in a place you had to walk along the bank of a creek for some distance to find a pool deep enough to get over your head much less practice a swimming stroke. He was right. It started a relationship in which he graciously taught me to swim well enough to compete in a decade's worth of triathlons but more importantly to foster a friendship that allowed me to observe and then postulate that **he is the finest man and most effective coach in a universe populated with amazingly talented men and women. Not just in the highly competitive field of world-class swimming...I mean any coach, in any sport.** There is a special place in heaven for Coach Reese!*

—RICK PERRY, US Secretary of Energy,
former Governor of Texas

*"Culture eats talent for breakfast" is just one of many riveting revelations to be found in this book. **If you are not already a devotee of Coach Reese's work, then this book will turn you into one! An illuminating, fast-paced read, we come to understand how Eddie became an iconic winning figure for athletes and coaches alike.** Touching on wide-ranging topics from training methodology to coaching philosophy to the importance of family, the question "Who is Eddie Reese" is skillfully highlighted by experienced historian and author, Coach Chuck Warner. The reader gets a front row seat to observe how humility and humor have defined Eddie Reese's winning career and made him a beloved figure in our sport. A highly recommended read for any swimming enthusiast!*

—KATHLEEN PRINDLE, Head Coach/Founder, PAQ Swimming
Board Vice-President, The American Swimming Coaches Association

# EDDIE REESE

## Coaching Swimming, Teaching Life

## CHUCK WARNER

*with Dana Abbott*

LUMINARE PRESS

WWW.LUMINAREPRESS.COM

*This book is dedicated to Eddie and Elinor Reese
and the Spirit with which they've lived their lives.*

*While a concise record of Eddie's coaching is merited, and shared even
more widely than it has been in the past, Elinor is a coach in her own
right. We are honored to be able to also share a bit of
Elinor Lasseter Reese's inspiring life.*

A significant portion of each book sale will be donated to
The University of Texas Eddie Reese & Kris Kubik
Men's Swimming & Diving Legacy Campaign.

*To donate directly to the endowment please go to*
www.thelonghornfoundation.com

# TABLE OF CONTENTS



──────── WHO IS EDDIE REESE? ────────



──────── HOW DOES EDDIE COACH? ────────

# Foreword

IT WAS MY PRIVILEGE TO BE THE ATHLETIC DIRECTOR AT
The University of Texas for thirty-two years. Eddie Reese was the
swim coach when I arrived and when I retired; he was the only
coach I did not hire. Nonetheless, he was a resource to me and the
entire athletic department from my first day to my last day on the
job. Perhaps the only door he has ever knocked on has been his
wife's, Elinor's. He never knocked on mine or anyone else's, but he
helped us all.

Before I got involved in athletic administration, my background
was in track, first as an athlete, then as a coach at Kansas State. We had
some success.* I always thought the research and insight into training
athletes in the sport of swimming was far ahead of where we were
in track. Consequently, I read every book that Doc Counsilman**
wrote. I essentially learned how to coach track from swim coaches.

In 1996 we made an exception to the normal procedure of waiting until a coach retires before inducting them into The University
of Texas Hall of Honor. We inducted Coach Reese while he was still
actively coaching because he represented everything that is good
about college athletics and The University of Texas athletic program.
It was evident that Eddie Reese and Kris Kubik were a team. So we
made the same exception for Coach Kubik and inducted him into
the UT Hall of Honor in 2011.

Within this book is a glimpse into how Eddie leads, and how
Kris supported him, to achieve their remarkable success. It is written and compiled by two of Eddie's former assistant coaches from
his first years at Texas. They were there every day to witness and participate in the early transformation of our program and have kept
close ties to Coach Reese in the years since. It is noteworthy that
Chuck Warner went on to coach three USA national teams himself
and became president of the largest swim coaching organization in

the world, the American Swimming Coaches Association (ASCA). Dana Abbott has had tremendous success in his own career and twice been elected president of the National Interscholastic Swimming Coaches Association (NISCA).

When young coaches search for a resource, just as I looked to Coach Counsilman, they would be wise to start here. When experienced coaches wonder what they're missing to maximize their athletes' and teams' potential, they could also look here for help.

I hope I'll be around for Eddie's retirement celebration. Elinor, can you help me with that?

DeLoss Dodds, *Athletic Director,*
*The University of Texas at Austin*
*1981–2013*

---

*In DeLoss Dodds' career as coach at Kansas State his athletes set world records and won eight Big 8 Team Championships.

**James E. "Doc" Counsilman published a landmark contribution to sports, "The Science of Swimming," in 1968. Doc was head coach for the 1976 USA Olympic Men's Swim Team, the most dominant Olympic swimming team in the modern era.

Authors' note: Prior to Dodds' hiring, Texas had won ten national team titles in its entire history. While he was athletic director, the Longhorn men won a remarkable fourteen national championships (the women's athletic department also produced twenty-six titles during this time).

 Chuck Warner

# Prologue

The ultimate success of a collegiate coach is measured in national team championships. The gold standard of NCAA coach-achievers includes the late UCLA coach John Wooden's record of ten basketball titles, Rod Dedeaux's eleven baseball titles at the University of Southern California, and Geno Auriemma's eleven championships (and counting) with the University of Connecticut's women's basketball team. The all-time NCAA team title leader is Anson Dorrance in women's soccer, at an amazing twenty-one titles at the University of North Carolina. In the professional ranks the leading coaches are Phil Jackson, with eleven NBA titles, Bill Belichick, with six Super Bowl wins, and Casey Stengel, with an unprecedented seven World Series Championships in baseball.

Down at The University of Texas at Austin, Edwin Charles "Eddie" Reese won his fourteenth team title in 2018 in one of America's preeminent sports, NCAA competitive swimming and diving. And, amazingly, Coach Reese's incoming freshman class of 2022 has been called one of the best in college history, in any sport.

The world measures individual excellence with Olympic medals. During Coach Reese's tenure, his swimmers have won thirty-nine gold, sixteen silver, and eight bronze medals at the Games. He turned down being a USA Olympic coach in 1984 and 2016 but otherwise has served in that capacity for America's most prolific Olympic squad in all the Games in between.

Ask Eddie what he loves about his work, and he'll tell you it's the relationships with people. Ask the people he has coached what they value most, and often they'll tell you, beyond even the winning, they treasure his effort to help them develop as a person. His compassion and caring for his swimmers, his friends, and even those he doesn't know personally is boundless. He has quietly reached out to help people in need for decades.

The trophies, medals, and honors that his teams and athletes have earned are at the top of anyone's list of athletic achievements from a coach's work. Is it possible that Eddie Reese's coaching skills, coupled with his humor and his kindness, could be unmatched in the history of athletics?

What we chronicle in the following pages is a glimpse into the teachings of Eddie Reese. Much of the wit and wisdom that permeates his life and his coaching is presented in his own words and penned center page and in bold print. Through these reiterations we intend for the reader to not only learn about Eddie Reese but to *feel the joy* that is ingrained in this coach's aura. As an opening sample, you might hear him greet one of his swimmers at a 6 a.m. practice with:

**It's good to see me.**

We hope this book will facilitate just that for you.

Important note: What appears in the text as class years—such as '04—indicates when a student-athlete's class would have graduated under a normal four- to five-year academic program. We have written the year this way to depict the final year they swam for Texas. The actual year of graduation is not always the same year.

 Chuck Warner

# Who Is
# Eddie Reese?

North Ridgewood School

*Second Grade*

# Mom Always Liked Me Best

*I'll retire when they stop laughing at my jokes.*

IN 2000, PRIOR TO HIS FOURTH STINT ON AN OLYMPIC coaching staff, Eddie prepared for the Sydney, Australia, Games as only he could:

**I took three years of Australian
but couldn't get the language.**

While some consider him a coaching genius and most appreciate his sense of humor, it's clear that these qualities go hand in hand for Eddie. Back in 1978 when Dana and I went to work as assistant coaches for Eddie at The University of Texas at Austin, each staff member completed a survey to discover what we valued most in our lives. For Eddie, the result was his ability to bring laughter to his interactions with others. Anyone who has spent even a little time with Coach Reese will testify to this truth.

The source of his wit came early in his life. Eddie's father, also called Eddie (Edwin Lightfoot Reese, Jr.), and his mother, Bettye, raised the future coach in a tiny two-bedroom house in Daytona Beach, Florida. His dad ensured that Eddie and his brother, Randy, five years younger, treated their mother with the utmost respect. The Reese men put her on a pedestal.

On that pedestal, however, Bettye Reese wielded a sharp wit. At breakfast one morning she looked at the weary eyes of her two teenage sons, who had been up late the night before, and said, "Your eyes look like goat droppings in a bowl of milk." She might discourage expletives with, "Be careful your mouth doesn't overload your pants."

Quips like this from his mom taught Eddie how to keep his flock in line with humor. Eddie's daughter Heather says, "Grandma was a small woman, but a laugh a minute … just hysterical."

Mr. Reese, Eddie's dad, had learned the value of being a competent swimmer in a traumatic way. Before they reached their teen years, three of his four younger brothers drowned in a river when the water rose more quickly than anticipated. Eddie's dad made sure he and Randy became proficient swimmers at an early age. Mr. Reese watched his own sons' initial swim instruction with keen interest, to be certain his boys would be safe around water.

Bettye Reese lived long enough to watch her sons grow into world-class swim coaches. In 2002 Eddie received one of swimming's highest accolades when he was inducted into the International Swimming Hall of Fame. Randy followed three years later, with a list of his own accomplishments, including winning NCAA team titles at the University of Florida and coaching numerous athletes to world records and Olympic medals.

In January of 1981 Eddie's Texas team competed with Randy's at the University of Florida. Dan Levin of *Sports Illustrated* wrote a marvelous article about the matchup (2/2/81):

*Bettye Reese sat high up in the packed stands at O'Connell Center in Gainesville, Fla., last Saturday night as No. 4-ranked Florida prepared to face top-ranked Texas in the teams' Civil War of swimming. She held allegiance to both sides, but more than that, she held allegiance to her sons: Coach Randy Reese of Florida, who had guided the Gators to victory in last year's war, and Coach Eddie Reese of Texas, who as coach at Auburn had given his brother's Gators their last dual meet defeat in 1978. "They're good boys," Bettye said. "They never fought as kids."*

*Or as adults, either, at least not seriously. But the dry Reese humor does provoke some skirmishing. On the eve of the meet, with Texas scheduled to show up for a last-minute workout, 34-year-old Randy was asked, "Will you wait here to see your brother tonight?" "No," he said, "but I'll drop by early to dump a load of chlorine in the pool." The next day, Eddie, 39, who, unlike Randy, is quick with a grin, gestured across the pool toward "that nasty-lookin' little fellow with the mustache over there."*

Levin completes his story of the competition between Florida and Texas, then concludes:

*Earlier, Bettye Reese had said, "They both belong to me, so all I'm saying is, 'May the best man win!'"*

*After Florida edged Texas she was asked, "Did the best man win?"*

*"Of course," she said. "And he lost, too."*

Eddie's humor and wit can range from self-deprecating comments about himself to friendly put-downs of his friends, disarming everyone around him. One example is when he was at a national professional conference. He passed a group of high school coaches he had known for years, and as he walked by their breakfast table he remarked:

**If a bomb went off under that table, the sport of swimming would fast-forward decades.**

Although he doesn't coach the women's team at The University of Texas he can brighten the day and bring a smile to the face of an awakening sleepy girl arriving for an early morning practice by calling her over and kindly suggesting:

**You've heard of a "hair do?" Well, that is a "hair don't."**

Eddie's humor knows few limits, especially with his athletes. In swimming a "bob" is taking a deep breath before submerging, exhaling, and then returning to the water's surface to repeat the action. Eddie has been known to tell his boys during a practice:

**Do three and a half bobs, and then you can go.**

*Eddie brings a smile to Dustin Wise and Ben Van Roekel.*

The coach knows how arduous competitive swimming is, and humor is his way of helping his athletes not only survive but excel in the rigorous training sessions:



Chuck Warner

**Swimming is too hard a sport for most people. You wake up earlier than you want. Work out longer than you want. Do it more frequently than you'd like. Don't have more than a few minutes to socialize during a workout. And you end your workout from where you started! Just a lot more tired.**

The coach frequently elicits his swimmers' smiles by explaining a challenging, and often complex, series of repeat swims. As he finishes the verbal instructions he will raise his arm above his head and hold up five fingers, visually indicating his instructions are to be performed for five rounds. After providing his swimmers enough time to fully absorb the almost insurmountable difficulty of completing five rounds, with a sparkle in his eyes Eddie will then say, "twice." The group's sigh of relief is often followed by a laugh.

It has been said that one of the greatest responsibilities we have as an adult is to become more of a child. Eddie Reese has fulfilled that responsibility often. Kris Kubik, his assistant coach for thirty-five years, shares this example:

*In the late '80s, we were swimming at the NCAA championship at IUPUI, and we stayed at the Hyatt Regency in downtown Indianapolis, which has an open-air atrium. As you walk outside your room there's a railing about six feet from the door, and when you look out over the railing, you can see all the way to the ground level. We had some people who were very skilled at making paper airplanes, and they would throw the paper airplanes out into the atrium.*

*The manager at the hotel called us and said, "Please stop throwing the paper airplanes." And as the manager called, Eddie was just making his. The airplane he made had all kinds of fancy wings and tears and angles in it.*

*He said, "Kris, call all the boys and tell them to look outside real quick."*

*And I said, "The manager just told us not to throw paper airplanes."*

*And Eddie said, "Just call 'em." So, at a specific time [the boys] crawled out and peeked over the railing. Eddie lofted his airplane and it hovered—and I don't want to exaggerate—for at least three minutes, just kind of floating up there in the atrium, above everything, before it sailed to the bottom. That's something I will never forget.*

College students sometimes have to leave practice early for class. Some coaches might acknowledge the departing swimmer with a frown. But Eddie chooses to play it a different way:

### Come back when you have no class.

Bill Robertson, a member of Eddie's inaugural team at Texas, says that Eddie could make a practice that might be over continue, and with laughter. "Go halfway out and halfway back and we're done," the coach might say.

The team would dutifully swim halfway across the pool and return to where they started. Eddie would say, "Sorry, you came *all* the way back, you were only supposed to come halfway back."

In Eddie's early years at Texas, the head women's coach was the famed Paul Bergen, who himself enjoyed a good laugh:

*There was the time when Ed and I were on deck during a morning training session in our summer season, when it was mentioned that we both had seen the same article in the paper about eating habits and diseases that were linked to body types. It concluded that thin people were more inclined to die of cancer, whereas overweight people were more inclined to die of heart disease.*

*Simultaneously we blurted out that we should go and have lunch at Baskin-Robbins after practice.*

In Eddie's first year at Texas, even the women's team learned that

 Chuck Warner

there was a place for fun. Toward the end of an autumn Saturday morning practice, the men had finished but the women continued. With no warning or announcement, Eddie jumped into the women's end of the pool, fully clothed, just to liven things up. Then the assistant coach, the late Stewart Rea, did the same off the starting block. Kris Kubik followed suit. Then diving coach Mike Brown, clad in full sweat suit, trotted a circle around the diving well, accompanied by the rising volume of both cheering teams. Brown sprinted up to the top of the ten-meter diving tower. To the amazement of all, he flipped and turned his way through thirty feet of air and splashed safely into the diving well.

*Diving Coach Mike Brown 1978*

A different kind of joy echoed inside the Texas Swimming Center that morning, one that reverberated through every athlete and coach. And it all began with Eddie's simple act of (strategically) becoming more of a child.

First-year UT swim parent Dave Thomas shared this story from one of his first experiences at a post-meet reception for Longhorn family and friends:

> *After a dual meet, it's common for Coach Reese to visit parents and alums in a reception area off the pool deck. As one could imagine, over the years of success after success the number of complimentary articles written about Eddie and the Texas Men's Swim Team have grown.*
>
> *A parent commented, "That was a nice article in The Alcalde [The University of Texas alumni magazine] about you and the men's team." Eddie's response: "I wrote it! My mother used to write articles like that about me. But I can't get Elinor [his wife] to do it."*

Some say that when one corner of the universe is tickled, the reverberation is such that in another far-off place there is laughter. Eddie Reese does a lot of figurative tickling each day, to a lot of people, but especially to his swimmers. By exercising his own brand of humor, he adheres not only to one of his own life purposes but also to one of the guiding tenets of his coaching philosophy:

**The key is to protect the swimmer's mind.**

 Chuck Warner

# CHAPTER 2

# Competitiveness

*I like to think I work pretty hard for my luck.*

WHILE RARELY ON PUBLIC DISPLAY, JUST BELOW THE surface of Eddie Reese's gracious, smiling demeanor resides the will of a fierce competitor.

In the fall of 1959 Eddie moved into his college dorm room at the University of Florida in Gainesville. He began his freshman year with an eye on engineering, hoping to build upon his ability to work with numbers. He changed his major, however, to physical education at about the same time he was becoming a key member of the varsity swim team. Increasingly uncomfortable with the minimal level of work required for the regular team practices, he began climbing over the wall at the UF pool after hours to train "extra" on his own. One of his favorite self-imposed challenges was to do 600-yard breaststroke pulls in order to improve what was at first a weak stroke.

*1963 (L-R) Coach Bill Harlan with team captains, Terry Green and Eddie Reese, and Coach Buddy Crone*

His competitive zeal and hard work were rewarded. In his senior year he became the first Florida swimmer to win five Southeastern Conference (SEC) Championship titles in a single season—the 200-yard breaststroke, the 200 and 400 individual medleys, and the 400 freestyle and 400 medley relays. And of perhaps even greater importance to Eddie, his team won the SEC Championships three consecutive years (1961–63).

Eighteen years later Coach Reese led Texas to its first NCAA Team Championships in 1981. John Smith '84, father of NCAA champion and American record holder Clark Smith '17, was a part of that first title team. John recalls listening to an exchange when one of the reporters who was gathered around Coach Reese asked, "You feel lucky?"

Eddie's response:

**I like to think I work pretty hard for my luck.**

You might say Coach Reese is a closet competitor. A prime example of Eddie's competitive fire stems from his younger years when the game of racquetball—about which he was incredibly passionate—was conducted in that closet. When he arrived at Texas in 1978 at the age of thirty-six, he soon found competition in his young assistant coach, Scott Hammond, age twenty-three.

Scott describes the experience:

*Anyone who wonders how Eddie Reese can be such a smiling, nice guy all the time, joking and appearing to always enjoy the present moment in a blissful, non-competitive way, has never truly competed with him as a partner, or head to head against him, in a small, enclosed four-walled court. Grab a racquet and smack a small blue rubber ball 110 mph and you begin to sense the intensity in that atmosphere.*

*During my two-year stint as an assistant coach, three to four days a week, Dave Snyder (UT Men's Tennis Coach), Tim Hamilton (UT Men's Assistant Track Coach), and Eddie and I met for our regular noon racquetball game. It was literally closed-in warfare. No-mercy, high-level racquetball and extremely competitive, with one of the four of us trash talking the whole way—it wasn't Dave, Tim, or me!*

*Eddie was good enough to play with any top-level [amateur] "A" player in Texas and many mid-level pros. He played with power, finesse, cunning, a cutthroat mentality that left nothing on the court, yet he could find a way to make us laugh, win or lose. Having him on your side in doubles was a treat because he increased your chance of winning the daily match, but he also made you a better player by allowing you to play your game. He was ferociously competitive, but in an internal way. He NEVER sulked over a loss, unlike some of us ... but he would razz you to death after a win.*

*His daily games went on for many years with the Texas coaches and he improved his game with age. When I left*

*Texas, if we were going to the same meet to recruit or were with our teams, we would be in contact and be sure to bring our racquetball gear, always finding time between prelims and finals to play at a YMCA or health club. For me, personally, there were not many things I have enjoyed as much in my life as the hundreds of matches of trash talking, competing, diving for balls, and trying to find a way to beat Eddie Reese in racquetball. When finished, the door closed and we walked off with a great workout, whether talking about swimming or life.*

Coach Pat Patterson became an occasional accomplice in duck hunting after Eddie succeeded him as head coach at UT. Pat describes the experience when he and a friend ventured off with Eddie: "It's amazing to me that three of us can shoot simultaneously as a flock of ducks fly overhead, and when three hit the ground Eddie claims it was he who shot them all."

**If everyone on my team gets significantly faster, then we're going to be hard to beat.**

That is a statement prior to the Big 12 Championships in 2018, following three straight UT NCAA team titles. Eddie is competitive for *his swimmers* and relishes watching their expression of delight after they swim faster than ever before.

Coaches almost never start at the top. When he first became head coach at Auburn, Eddie's team was at the bottom of the conference, and when Coach Reese arrived in Austin he also had to work his way through some challenging times. During the first season, he once called the entire team out onto the pool deck because of their poor training performance, sat them down, and said with intensity, "I am prepared to lose anyone but me!"

*Eddie's inaugural Texas squad 1978–79*

I have known Coach Reese about forty-three years and only heard him use expletives twice. I especially remember the competitive pain associated with the first experience.

Eddie's Auburn team finished second at the 1978 NCAA Championships, but when he moved to Texas the team was not able to compete at nearly that level. The 1979 NCAA Championships were held at Cleveland State University. Eight national-class swimmers that had transferred to Texas to swim with Eddie were not permitted to compete for the Longhorns their first year, due to the NCAA transfer rules. Superstars Scott Spann and Kris Kirchner were among the eight that stayed back in Austin, training with Kris Kubik.

Thanks only to some diving points, we finished tied for twenty-first. We would have placed much lower if not for the divers, as the swimmers only managed one point amongst them.

Toward the end of that '79 competition, Eddie and I were walking down a hall with no one around, when Eddie vented. "Next year we are going to !#!&!" I was surprised to hear the series of expletives from one of the people that I admire most in the world. But it testified to the intensity of his competitive fire.

Just one year later (1980) the UT team finished second. Since that time, his teams have placed first or second an incredible twenty-five times.

**We have a great group of kids. They know they
go fast here [conference] and faster at NCAAs.**

To compete at the highest level of the sport, it's essential that coaches first find talented athletes that fit their program and then sell them on who they are and what their school offers (that others might not). It's an arduous process, especially since it requires working each year with perhaps dozens of seventeen-year-old very young adults and their often anxious parents. Yet over the course of his career, Eddie Reese has been—and continues to be—one of America's most traveled recruiters. Beyond his unquenchable desire to field a competitive team, it is Eddie's genuine enjoyment of "swimming people" that enables him to spend the necessary time away from home. Unlike a combined men's and

                     Chuck Warner

women's team where five coaches can recruit, as a single-gender sport team only two swim coaches are allowed to recruit. Thus, Eddie's staff has primarily been Kris Kubik and himself.

**When I go fishing, I like to catch the biggest, the smallest, the first, the last, and the most.**

This means, for example, in a championship competition Eddie wants to be sure his swimmers are prepared in every way and swim fast at every session.

**You don't sleep through these things. You come here and you experience more pain. I went to bed at 1 a.m. [Friday morning] looking at the psych sheets and woke up at 4:15. I was so worried [Stanford] would score 2,000 points in the backstroke.**

Doug Gjertsen '90 quickly became indoctrinated into the competitive nature of his college coach:

*"[My freshman year] I watched the Cardinal do that #$!@ [victory] cheer in our pool and I almost got physically ill. I swore to never let that happen again while our class had the ability to change it."*

*Doug Gjertsen, 1988 and 1992 Olympian, Gold and Silver Medalist*

For more than two decades, Texas and Stanford "enjoyed" a fierce rivalry at the NCAA Championships. As Josh Davis '94 liked to say, "I love beating Stanford." But the Cardinal won their fair share too.

In the fall of 1988 Mark Schubert took over the reins of the women's program at Texas. When it comes to club swimming in the United States, Mark is the undisputed king of national team championships. He won a record forty-four at Mission Viejo (CA) and added nine more at Mission Bay (FL). By 1988 a great many of his swimmers had won a slew of Olympic gold medals, and as a result Mark had traveled the world as a coach-member of too many USA national teams to count.

Mark shares this story:

*I walked into the Texas Swimming Center for my first practice. I hadn't been able to get my Texas gear yet, so I didn't have a University of Texas shirt to wear. I thought I would be "the cool USA national coach" and wear my USA gear. I had on a red USA Swimming shirt. I walked onto the pool deck and without a welcome or introduction, I heard Eddie's voice say, "You're going to learn to hate that color." I never wore red again, that season, or ever.*

**The rewards have nothing to do with winning the race, and everything to do with swimming fast.**

Perhaps it's the view of competing with oneself to find the fastest swimming inside of you that keeps the competitive pressures in appropriate perspective for both Coach Reese and his swimmers, providing them with an unshakable foundation that enables them to perform at their very best, when it counts the most.

*Townley Haas Olympic Gold Medalist 2016*

**Personally, I try to get better at
everything I do every year.**

Science says the entire cellular makeup of a human being is replaced
every seven years. As our time on earth extends, we have the choice
to strive for personal growth mentally and physically. Like all of us,
Eddie Reese isn't physically the same person he was years ago, yet he
makes sure that his mind continues to grow. And as he will gladly
admit, with that passing of time perhaps a little of his internal fire
has been traded for a more philosophical view of competition. In
an interview in 2018, he had this to say:

> **Now when we compete, we're still as competitive as can
> be when that gun goes off, but afterward you shake hands
> and are happy for the winner. I heard something years
> ago: "At the end of the contest you should not be able to
> tell the winners from the losers." I realize that might be
> impossible. But it sure sounds good.**

                    Chuck Warner

# Chapter 3

# Recruiting

*All I recruit is distance per stroke.*

When Eddie took over the head coaching reins at Auburn University in 1972, the team was dismal. The previous year Auburn had not had a single individual swimmer finish in the top sixteen places (to score a point) at the Southeastern Conference Championships. When his wife, Elinor, asked him who the best recruits in the country were, Eddie rattled off the names of some high school stars. Some were Olympians. Eddie added, "They're not going to come to Auburn. We need to build a program first."

Elinor pressed the issue, "How do you know until you ask?"

Eddie never forgot his wife's message and used her confidence to build his own. By that time, Elinor Reese had appointed herself president of the Eddie Reese Fan Club. As she saw it, other schools had no chance where her husband was concerned. "How could you recruit against such a nice guy?"

One of Coach Reese's many talents is finding swimmers with the potential to improve, often dramatically, under his system. One of many examples was the diminutive (5'7") Gary Schatz, who was swimming in relative obscurity in a Midland, Texas, high school. Eddie saw his potential and developed it. As a result Gary helped Auburn climb into the top ten at the NCAA Championships in Eddie's third year with the War Eagles.

As Eddie's reputation for swimmer development grew, so did the strength of subsequent recruiting classes. The freshman class that entered in his fifth year included three prep school stars from brother Randy's program at the Episcopal School of Jacksonville: Olympian Billy Forrester, future World Champion David McCagg, and Scott Spann. The following year future Hall of Famer and Olympic gold medalist Rowdy Gaines became a War Eagle as well. Just six years after Eddie Reese became a college head coach for the first time, his team finished second at the 1978 NCAA Championships.

Now it was Eddie being recruited. Darrell Fick '78, star swimmer (400 IM) on the 1978 University of Texas team, remembers:

*We found out that Coach Patterson was going to retire, and we [The University of Texas] were looking for a new coach. I had five quarters and went to the pay phone. I put them in and had five minutes. I called Eddie. He said, "I know who you are." I told Eddie that Coach Patterson was retiring and that The University of Texas is a great place to be.*

*Eddie said, "Elinor is not going to like this. We just built a house."*

When Texas Athletic Director and former head football coach Darrell Royal asked the retiring Patterson for advice on a new coach,

 Chuck Warner

he suggested Eddie. Coach Reese flew off to Austin to interview for the position. Coach Royal picked up Eddie at the airport.

Eddie: "I guess you guys are pretty serious about this."

Coach Royal: "Why do you say that?"

Eddie: "Because I'm sure you would rather be out playing golf today."

*Eddie and Coach Pat Patterson 2015*

Coach Pat Patterson shares what took place when he joined Eddie and Darrell Royal for dinner:

*We went to Cisco's Mexican restaurant on East 6th street.*

*You could tell Eddie had never had jalapeño peppers before— his upper lip was sporting a line of perspiration and sweat was running down his temple, which he kept wiping with his napkin—but he kept telling Darrell how good it was.*

*My daughter Christie tells me when he got back to Auburn he was heard to say, "they tried to kill me at both ends" [possibly*

Eddie returned home and told Elinor, "Everything is bigger and better in Texas." Soon thereafter they moved with their two little girls, Heather and Holly, to Austin, Texas.

*The Texas Swimming Center opened in 1977. The persistence of former coach Tex Robertson was essential to its construction.*

Phil Nenon was one of the many Auburn swimmers who considered making the move as well. Here is how he remembers the decision:

*I must admit the mischief we were up to for entertainment in the remote town of Auburn, Alabama, in retrospect makes me think some of us needed to make a move. Eddie had announced he was going to Texas. We were at a meet in Austin and my "recruiting trip" to stay at Auburn was an invitation to go to dinner with newly named Auburn Head Coach Richard Quick. Richard took me to Cisco's. The Mexican food was sensational. I was sold! I made the move to Texas.*

The reputation Coach Reese had established at Auburn for helping

 Chuck Warner

swimmers get faster enabled him to attract the interest of many of the country's best swimmers. Texas unseated Southern Methodist University (SMU) as the flagship of collegiate swimming programs in the Lone Star state. The coaching, clubs, and swimmers within Texas progressed in earnest. While Eddie continued to recruit all over the country, more and more great high school swimmers chose to stay home in Texas where they could prosper and also receive the benefit of in-state tuition.

Bryan Jones '00 grew up in College Station, Texas. "I grew up seeing those 'Don't Mess With Texas' t-shirts all over the pool deck at meets. Like many of my friends, I wanted to be a part of that program."

Coach Kubik shares this story in a splendid article by Chris O'Connell, published in 2018 by *The Alcalde*:

*In 1986, Highland Park High School senior Shaun Jordan, BA '93, MBA '97, was in Austin for the state swimming championships. A self-described late-bloomer and a lightly recruited swimmer, Jordan had a disappointing third-place finish in the 100-yard freestyle event. He saw it as the end of his swimming career. Reese saw a beautiful stroke.*

*"We have to sign him," Kubik remembers him saying from the stands.*

*Kubik called Jordan, who had planned to come to UT anyway and pledge a fraternity. Kubik asked if he would meet with Reese to talk about swimming, and the recent high school graduate agreed. Jordan would be in town the following week for a pre-rush event and would be happy to meet with him.*

*"So, I pick him up in front of some house, he's got the khaki pants and button-down shirt, totally prepped out," Kubik says. "He talks to Eddie and Eddie says, 'Why don't you swim for a year, and if you don't like it, you can always pledge a fraternity.'"*

*Jordan joined the team as a walk-on with a book scholarship, redshirting his freshman year. "I was growing a bunch, getting run over by guys who were best in the world," Jordan says. "I trusted him completely. Eddie took really good care of me. He changed my life."*

*Jordan went on to become one of only two swimmers in Texas history to be part of four national championship teams. He also won gold medals in the 1988 and 1992 Olympics as a member of the US freestyle relay team.*

*Jordan says that as he fell under Reese's spell, he became obsessed with getting faster. It just took the right amount of care and instruction from his coach to get him to that next level. "He was nuanced in what I needed and what other guys needed," Jordan says. "He's not throwing everyone in one hopper and turning a crank. He has such a touch and such a sense of what the athlete needs."*

*Shaun Jordan, 1991 Team Captain*

**There are plenty of people that can be great swimmers, but you have to pick the right ones or it will be a mess.**

John Leonard, long-time executive director of the American Swimming Coaches Association, once asked, "Does Eddie recruit respectful gentlemen or do they become that way during their time at Texas?"

The answer is he tries to do the former but often achieves the latter.

While Eddie has had success in molding talented young college swimmers, over time he has also been able to increasingly fill his team with athletes that are focused academically and possess high character. As the Texas program became dominated by this type of individual, it held even greater attraction for like-minded high school swimmers.

Olympic gold medalist Garrett Weber-Gale '07 offers this insight into Coach Reese's counsel: "He reminds us that we're the same person we were before we had success. We should be proud but not righteous."

His athletes respect a favorite Reese saying:

**I'd rather be thought a fool than
open my mouth and prove it.**

Reese's network of coaching friends around the country grew, and they often pointed out or recommended individuals they thought had the ability, desire, and character to swim fast in his program at Texas.

From Bryan Collins '11:

*When Eddie was recruiting me in high school, he told me he was coming to watch me at a meet one particular weekend. I couldn't find him in the stands but assumed he was there some-where. I was very nervous for him to watch but also excited—I went best times by a lot in the 500 free and 200 back.*

*I called Eddie that night, excited to talk to him. "Bryan, I made a mistake." He had confused his schedule and thought my meet was the next weekend, so he never actually saw me swim before I showed up in Austin my freshman year.*

*Eddie later told me he would have never recruited me if he had seen me swim in high school. (This was actually a compli-ment, as the context was I turned out to be an okay swimmer.)*

*"This is what it's like to have talent"—Eddie points at Brian Wilson. "This is what it's like to not have talent"—Eddie points at me.*

*"Bryan C., we should have you neutered so you can't pass on your breaststroke." When Bryan asked about trying sprinting, Eddie quipped, "You will forever be a snail."*

But Bryan Collins became an All American and school record holder in the 400-yard individual medley.

### The best people are in swimming.

An abundance of swimmers have come to swim for Eddie Reese from odd circumstances and limited backgrounds. The overall personal benefits in this one are special:

Ian Carbone swam five to six days a week for an hour in a small Y program in Bar Harbor, Maine, with no training competition. His breaststroke times in his junior year of high school of :59 for 100 yards and 2:10 in the 200 were nowhere near what was common for a Texas freshman.

I reconnected with Ian's dad, my old friend Bob, at a mutual friend's memorial service outside Austin. At the event we discussed Ian's college prospects. Duquesne University had offered him some athletic aid. I confirmed that it seemed like a good choice.

In January Bob called to tell me that Duquesne had dropped their men's team. As the months went by and the April scholarship signing period drew near we discussed his new top choice—and really only choice—the University of Denver.

At the National Y Championships in April 2010, I was impressed watching Ian swim his best times of :57 in the 100 breast and 2:05 in the 200. The day after the meet I received a text from Bob showing a picture of Ian at 6'5" tall. I called Bob to learn more about Ian and whether being a little fish in a big pond could work for him. Then I asked, "Would you mind if I called Eddie Reese at Texas?"

 Chuck Warner

Bob was stunned but was all for it. I called Eddie and told him about Ian. He said, "I need a breaststroker and he sounds like my kind of guy [limited background with lots of potential]. He's a junior, right?"

I said, "No, he's a senior planning to visit Denver in four days then make his decision."

Eddie said, "I'll call him tonight."

Ian Carbone flew, with his mom, to Denver for a Friday-Saturday visit and then straight to Austin to visit Texas. The only return flight to Maine that his mom could find at the last minute gave them a very early flight back home from Austin. At 4:30 a.m. Eddie Reese picked up Ian and his mother and drove them to the airport. Ian Carbone had a wonderful four years at Texas. His senior year he split 52.6 in the 100 breaststroke on a medley relay.

Best of all, for those four years Bob Carbone could visit Ian and spend time with our friend's widow and five children, reminding each other how the sport of swimming had always brought them together.

After Ian's senior season, Eddie summed up for Ian's dad: "He overcame from where he came."

The 2018 recruiting class (UT Class of 2022; please see Appendix I on page 153) was the product of not only Eddie's work but that of his two new assistant coaches, Wyatt Collins and volunteer Chase Kreitler. After the incredible class was announced, Eddie commented:

**The best recruiting class in history … in any sport.**

# Coaching College Men

*I've coached eighteen to twenty-two-year-olds
my whole life.*

EXCEPT FOR ONE SEASON COACHING HIGH SCHOOL, EDDIE Reese has spent his entire career coaching college men. After earning his degree at Florida in 1963, he stayed on as a graduate assistant for two more years. In looking for his first full-time position he landed in Roswell, New Mexico, when the school system offered Elinor a position. They found a spot for Eddie to both teach elementary school and coach high school swimming. After one year the Reeses returned to the University of Florida, where Eddie served as an assistant coach from 1966 to 1972. Following that he became head coach for six seasons at Auburn, 1972–78, and ultimately head coach of Texas in the spring of 1978.

 Chuck Warner

One of his "volunteer" positions is to coach most everyone around him. This role has included teaching the folks walking from the parking lot to the Texas Swimming Center how to say hello to each other. He also serves in an official capacity instructing young swimmers at the Longhorn Swim Camp that he developed at Texas.

After arriving at the UT campus in 1978, Eddie met his new swimmers and mixed landscaping with team bonding. Doug Harlow and the team got to know their new coach a little better this way:

> *After Eddie moved to Austin he invited the team over to his house for pizza one summer evening. It turned out to be an unscheduled dry land exercise workout—laying eight pallets of sod by hand in the front and back yards of his new house. Then we got pizza and were introduced to (the game) four-square—all was good.*

*In 1982 Eddie coped with his NCAA Medley Relay Champion's snake hobby. (L-R, Nevid, Britt, Eric Finical, Paulus) This python wasn't the one they smuggled on a plane from California in a pillow case ... was it?*

**Teaching physical education in the elementary school has more than qualified me to coach college swimmers.**

*A weekend activity of crawling through a two-mile, eighteen-inch cave.*
*L-R, World Champion Nick Nevid, American Record Holder*
*Clay Britt, Olympic Gold Medalist Steve Lundquist,*
*World Record Holder William Paulus, Greg Hanigan*

Coaching college men can be challenging for many reasons. Among these is the fact that eighteen-year-old boys arriving at college, often for their first extended experience away from home, can be eager to experiment with all their social opportunities. This, as many of us have discovered, can lead to less-than-stellar decision making. Five-time Olympic gold medalist Aaron Peirsol remembers his coach of almost ten years saying:

**Better to be a smart ass than a dumb ass.**

Eddie has had great patience with the former but not so much with the latter. His rapier wit can fill a room with laughter or corral a youth gone astray and generally keep him in his place. But sometimes that's not enough. Young college men (and older ones too) can do dumb things.

Rob Jones '87 explains:

> *I believe every swimmer who has been graced with Eddie's knowledge has experienced the formidable "Back-of-the-Arm-Grab," sometimes affectionately referred to as "The Claw." Always subtle. Not a strong grip, but always with purpose. It got your attention. It was always effective. And it always made you stop what you were doing and listen to whatever Eddie was telling you.*
>
> *To me, the Back-of-the-Arm-Grab sums up what Eddie is all about: not a yeller, but he could get your attention very quickly. And you listened.*

Dale Rogers UT MBA '12 adds:

> *Eddie is the only person that could control grown men or get their undivided attention by grabbing them by the elbow ... His swimmers will know exactly what I'm talking about.*

Coach Reese knows that treating people with kindness and respect reaps being treated with kindness and respect. Bill Stapleton '87 ('88 Olympian) looks back:

> *I remember the Eddie "claw" on the bicep when he was pissed or that look in his eyes when you let him down. No one wants to disappoint Eddie. That's what makes him great. It's about respect and honor with him, and we all want him to believe in us.*

Scott Mactier '82 was a part of Eddie's first team at Texas and describes his experience this way:

*He taught us about focus, dedication, what it takes to be a world champion, and even though I wasn't one, I was treated as if I could be.*

Another common practice he employs is waving his hand in a slapping motion while saying:

**Why don't you walk into this?**

Administering discipline might be Eddie Reese's least favorite part of coaching. College swimmers face many temptations, ranging from not going to classes regularly to leading a night life that is counterproductive to training. Kris Kubik has been a close ally in not only coaching swimming but teaching young men responsibility to themselves and team.

Katie Arris-Wilson '12, a member of the Texas women's team and an inductee into The University of Texas Women's Athletics Hall of Honor, shares this insight:

*In 2013 I was on deck speaking with Eddie about his team. He told me he had a few guys who were not making good decisions outside the pool and, as a result, were bringing the team down. He told me he sat down with one of them (who happened to be one of the fastest guys on the team) and told him that he needed to grow up. And then he said, "And you are not going to grow up at Texas." In other words, he was kicked off the team.*

*Eddie knows that the key to success is TEAM and he knew when he needed to get rid of someone who was negatively impacting the team, after other measures to correct the behavior had not worked.*

**It was important to do it, for him and for us.**

Katie re-visited UT in 2016 and had this experience:

*I was at the Working Exes for Texas Swimming (WETS) ban-*

　　　　Chuck Warner

*quiet and Eddie was talking about having won the National Championships in March. In all his characteristic humility he said, "The truth is, these guys make me look like a lot better coach than I am. They make all the right decisions outside of the pool. When you have a group of guys who make good decisions outside the pool, they make everything we do as coaches with them in the pool and in the weight room work a lot better."*

*He communicated this in a way as if to imply he was lucky to have a group of men who came together and made good decisions. I knew that was not always the case because I remembered the conversation from 2013.*

Every coach knows that team culture is a key to success, but few actually know how to make the tough decisions to create that culture. Eddie clearly knows this, yet he gives the credit to his guys, not to himself.

**All over the world people ask me what is the
magic to our success? You are the magic.**

Those are the words to his team before their first practice after the Rio Olympics in the fall of 2016. Eddie explained that the swimmers are ninety percent responsible for their success and the coaches only ten percent responsible. Some young men take a little more of the professed ten percent than others.

Robert Bogart '98:

*Eddie is one of the best human beings I know. For as witty as he can be, it pales in comparison to his wisdom and patience. I have no idea how I made it through five years there without being canned. Moreover, I have no idea where I'd be today without the work that he put into me. Aside from so many life-changing lessons that he taught in the context of swimming, he gave me the best five years in the sport that any aspirational young man could dream of.*

**Swimming has the best people: swimmers,
coaches, and some parents.**

Coaching college-age swimmers can be a challenge, but coaches encounter unique situations with athletes of every age; some even have parents acting on their behalf as assistant coaches. In 1981 I called Eddie and expressed my frustration with my coaching position. I fondly recall his words, which might help any coach, teacher, or parent smile and keep their perceived troubles in perspective:

**The only people that are completely
happy live in a mental institution.**

    Chuck Warner

# CHAPTER 5

# Eddie's Coach

*There are three kinds of smart:*
*Book, which is learned...*
*Intelligence, with which you're born...*
*Wisdom, which you marry.*

*Elinor's 21st birthday*

PASSION AND PERSISTENCE ARE ESSENTIAL TO GREAT coaching; with the addition of perspective, a great coach becomes a great teacher.

Each evening Coach Reese makes the drive from the Jamail Texas Swimming Center to his family home in the suburbs of Austin. During that time the coach makes the transition from the noise of coaching college students to the peaceful presence of his wife. At a park on his route home he often spots a family of deer, "a sight I never get tired of." A welcome call from one of his girls might interrupt his solitude.

When he arrives home, the best part of his life is often there to greet him. Elinor has been his best friend and companion for more than fifty-five years. There is no doubt in Eddie's mind that Elinor Reese's willingness to devote her life to help others facing critical circumstances dwarfs what most swim coaches do on a day-to-day basis. Each evening, catching up with his wife's day puts Eddie's work life in its proper perspective.

Elinor Reese's faithful service to the poor and homeless is an exquisite counterbalance to the elite achievements of one of history's greatest coaches.

Given their different family backgrounds, Eddie and Elinor don't seem like a match made in heaven. Elinor's father, J. Haywood Lasseter, was the proverbial self-made man. Although he never went to college, he worked his way from selling shoes, to selling furniture, to becoming an interior designer. He eventually became the first president of American Interior Designs. J. became so successful at his trade that his work included designing and decorating President Harry Truman's "Little White House" in Key West.

Elinor's mom, Elsiemae, was sent back to England, where her parents were born, to go to school. At age fourteen Elsiemae begged for the transatlantic education to stop; it did, but so did all her formal schooling. Elsiemae did not pursue a career outside the home in Miami but worked to raise her children through Elinor's high school years.

Determined that Elinor should have a better life, Elinor says, "My father worked really hard getting us into society. ... I was asked to be a debutante and went to all the deb parties ... He worked so hard to get [us] into the blue book in the Miami social scene ... My parents were very big party people, [they were always] entertaining people."

**Mom was on a pedestal.**

In comparison, Eddie's dad managed a hardware store and then owned a gas station. He didn't earn a college degree either. Mr. Reese was a very kind and polite man who modeled an exceptional quality for his son: treating his wife Bettye with the utmost respect.

During her high school years, Elinor attended "proper" upscale social functions and, trying to fit in, could frequently be spotted with a glass of "spirits" and a cigarette. "My dad told me, 'don't sneak-smoke. If you're going to smoke, smoke in front of us; if you're going to drink, drink in front of us.' That's the way I was raised." Elinor's parents wanted her to marry a successful man from an upper-class family.

Elinor entered the University of Florida in the fall of 1959 and majored in physical education. At the start of her junior year, she noticed a handsome young man in her social dance class. It was Eddie. "He was so cute! I stalked him," she jokes. "I looked up all his information in our yearbook. And he knew nothing about me."

Elinor wanted to make sure Eddie noticed her, so each day after the dance class she pretended she had a class across campus in the same direction Eddie was walking. Then she'd come back to where her class really was—in the same building as dance. Elinor's persistence included timing her visits to the bank to be there when Eddie went in to take out spending money.

**She could beat me at every game,
including running tree to tree.**

Swimming was the one skill that Eddie knew more about, and he proceeded to teach Elinor how to swim butterfly. Most of all, though, it was his humor that charmed her. At Elinor's dormitory each student had an open mail box. Each day Eddie would leave her a note. She's saved most them.

**Roses are red,
Violets are blue,
When I think of happiness,
I think of myself!**

On their first date Elinor forgot her purse. Looking back, she considers it a blessing because her cigarettes were in it. "That would have been our first and last date," she says. "Those were the days of Elvis and the ducktails, and the Pat Boones, and the good guys wore white hats, and the bad guys drank. Eddie was one of the good guys."

Once Eddie started telephoning her, he made it a lifelong daily habit. He generally starts the conversation with, "Hey, good-lookin'!"

While Eddie's middle-class background was not what her father had envisioned for his daughter, he accepted her decision to marry Eddie. Exacerbating her parents' concerns about Elinor's security was the fact that, although her father was a success in his creative art, he wasn't a good business person. During her college years he declared bankruptcy.

The aspirations Elinor's parents had once held for her future appeared to be in trouble. Eddie didn't have the money for a ring, and Elinor's family had little for a wedding. Nevertheless, they planned their wedding for Thursday, August 15, 1963. Eddie hustled back to town after a swim meet for the big day, and they found that the newly constructed apartment they were going to rent was still without electricity, heat, or water. Undaunted, they proceeded with the wedding. The guests toasted the occasion with silver champagne glasses, a gift from Elinor's aunt. Eddie joined the formality but with a non-alcoholic drink in his glass.

 Chuck Warner

*August 15, 1963, Wedding Day*

After exchanging marriage vows on Thursday, Elinor began her teaching position at Gainesville High School on Monday morning. The young couple remained in Gainesville for two years, while Eddie earned his master's degree and served as a graduate assistant coach with the Gators. He also learned important lessons about taking care of athletes from his coaches Buddy Crone and Bill Harlan.

**They were great, positive coaches and just all-around decent human beings.**

With his master's degree in hand, Eddie typed letters to colleges, seeking a position as a swim coach. He received several rejections, including one from a private academy in Roswell, New Mexico. Elinor, however, was hired as a physical education teacher in Roswell. To secure her recruitment to their school, the administration found a teaching position for Eddie in an elementary school, as well as a high school coaching position.

A year later Eddie and Elinor returned to the University of Florida, where Eddie served as assistant coach for the next six years while also teaching tennis, handball, and volleyball. Although only in his mid-twenties he accepted a large degree of responsibility for designing and implementing the swim team's training. In 1967 Holly was born. In 1969 Heather joined the family, too.

Major changes took place in the extended Reese family in the early 1970s. In 1972 Eddie was hired as head coach at Auburn University. In 1975 both of their fathers passed on. Although her dad was only sixty-five when he passed away, Elinor was pleased that he had been able to witness Eddie's advancement in his career. With the loss of Elinor's father, her mom needed to earn a living. Elsimae went to work in a hospital gift shop with a savings program; the shop would match whatever its employees saved. Through her thrift and planning, Elsiemae supported herself until she passed on at age ninety-seven.

Elinor was hired to teach physical education classes at Auburn, which helped the family income. Despite traveling and spending time on the phone with recruits, Eddie made a point of putting his family first. Occasionally he would join Holly or Heather at school for lunch. He jokes, "By the time they reached high school, that wasn't so well received." As the girls remember it, when he was home he was on the floor playing with them and at every big dance recital, softball game, or school event.

Holly and Heather's parents required them to participate in a sport of their choice but didn't want to nudge them toward swimming, given their father's work. At a sleepover a friend of Heather's invited her to join her at a swim practice the next morning; Heather liked it. Holly and Heather joined competitive swimming, which they continued through their high school years.

Elinor and Eddie built their dream house in Auburn, with a pond on their property where Eddie could fish every day. He had no desire to move anywhere, although the University of North Carolina and Texas were schools he admired. When the

　　　　　Chuck Warner

team finished second at the 1978 NCAA Championships, Texas called, and the Reese family was off to Austin.

*An early year of the Longhorn Swim Camp. Over its forty years under Coach Reese, it has grown to serve over 20,000 swimmers, including some that eventually earned a spot on a USA Olympic Team, such as Missy Franklin, Tom Wilkins, Elizabeth Beisel, Gary Hall Jr., Brad Bridgewater and Allison Schmidt.*

When the Reese foursome arrived in Texas their house wasn't ready. With the Longhorn Swim Camp about to start, the family moved into the Jester Dorm to live and host the campers. Heather recalls, "I thought moving to Texas meant we'd be riding horses to school. That didn't work out, but how could you beat being eight years old and living in a college dorm? That was the best!"

*Eddie and Heather at the 1980 Southwest Conference Championships*

Eventually they moved into their house, and Elinor elected to stay at home so she could help the family adjust to their new community. Soon she realized that their family needed her to earn an income. She took a job at the St. Edwards Health & Fitness Center, then began teaching "body & soul" classes at the Presbyterian Church at which the family had become members. Elinor worked on the attendees' bodies, while the assistant pastor took care of the souls. Through the experience, Elinor was exposed to the pastor's Bible studies, which prompted her to think more deeply about Scripture.

If it was typical for a husband in the 1970s to expect dinner on the table when he arrived home from work, one would think this would be especially true in the South. "Eddie never asked anything of me in that way," Elinor says. "If there was no dinner ready he would just say, 'I'm happy with a sandwich anyway.' I might have a thousand things to ask of him or be critical of, but he never had one of me."

**The key is marrying the right person.**

That is a statement uttered by both Eddie and Elinor Reese. Simple in concept? Yes. Always easy? No.

One test came when Elinor found herself in the frustrating

                    Chuck Warner

position of carrying out most of the home chores, including mowing the lawn and doing their taxes. As the couple worked through their expectations, they realized that, as Elinor says, "We could pay anyone to do those tasks, but Eddie was (and is) a superb father and husband. You can't hire someone to do that." Their commitment to each other, to their marriage, and to communication prompted them to focus first on what was and is most important: each other and their family. They found people to handle the chores, and Eddie learned to enjoy some of Elinor's hobbies, such as dance and the theatre. Elinor continued in her role as president of the Eddie Reese Fan Club.

Eddie emulated his father by keeping Elinor on a pedestal, giving her his complete support. Heather explains, "My parents are amazing. When you see them at one of our sporting events they are holding hands or rubbing each other's shoulders—still so much in love."

As Holly and Heather entered their high school years, Elinor's intention to serve others grew. One day someone called her from the church and asked if she would like to help distribute day-old donuts to people on the street. She and the youth director's wife drove the streets looking for homeless people. "At first I wanted to just throw the donuts [to them] out the window. These guys were standing on street corners, [covered with] tattoos."

As the two women began engaging the self-segregated groups of African-Americans, Hispanics, and Caucasians, however, they became acutely aware of the racial divisions between the groups. Each group would say, "We're okay, but look out for those guys!"

As Elinor grew more familiar with the individuals among the various homeless groups, she listened to their concerns. When the subject of bathing came up, she helped arrange transportation to a local Y to meet that need. Then she added lunch at the church, arranged for haircuts, medicine, clothing closets, laundry assistance, and more.

Elinor soon became head of the Foundation for the Homeless Ministry. She worked to arrange services donated by local businesses. Then they recruited the involvement of other churches.

Subtly she encouraged Eddie to help as well.

Eddie Reese is protective of Elinor. "If I go off to the grocery store and am not back about the time I said I would be, he will often call to make sure I'm okay."

One day Elinor received a call from a couple that had briefly lived with the Reeses. The couple was in a predicament and asked Elinor if she could give them a ride to the place they had found for temporary housing.

When Elinor agreed, Eddie said, "You just jump as soon as they call you?"

Elinor said, "Well then, come with me."

He did.

They drove to the woods where the couple was living. Eddie stayed in the car while Elinor located the couple. When they appeared, all their possessions were in a brown paper bag. The Reeses drove them to a motel, and as they left Eddie asked Elinor, "What are they going to eat?"

Elinor knew from experience that fast food restaurants frequently disposed of unsold food in dumpsters. With that in mind she said, "I don't know, there's probably dumpsters around!"

Aghast, Eddie retorted, "Elinor!" Eddie drove to a Pizza Hut nearby and went through the salad bar, putting together a healthy, nutritious dinner, which they then brought to the couple at their motel.

Elinor developed friendships with many homeless people. She helped a man named Houston get off heroin. Eventually Houston decided to give up alcohol as well and enter in-patient rehab. Elinor was thrilled and, with the help of some friends in the legal profession, got Houston admitted to an institution. However, he would have to wait two weeks for a bed.

When Elinor shared the problem with Eddie, Coach Reese agreed to have Houston stay at their home for those two weeks. Elinor and Eddie scurried around their home, cleansing it of mouth wash that contained alcohol, mini liquor bottles they had kept for guests (untouched for ten years), and anything else that might tempt Houston.

　　　　　　　Chuck Warner

A week or so later Heather called from the University of Florida, where she was attending college. Her mom explained that Houston was using her shower. Heather said, "You have a homeless person in my shower?"

Elinor tried to reassure her. "Honey, it's okay. He's sleeping in your room."

Houston not only made it through rehab but also attended Heather's wedding at the Barton Creek Country Club.

After Elinor had devoted just over a year to running the foundation for the church, it had grown to such a degree that her duties shifted to writing grants for financial support. She didn't feel trained to perform such duties, so she stepped down. Fortunately, as Coach Reese's success with both Texas and the Longhorn Swim Camp brought increasing financial rewards, Elinor's income wasn't as important to the family's finances. After leaving the foundation Elinor volunteered at hospice and with AIDS patients.

Both Elinor and her daughters sing the chorus, "Money has never mattered to Eddie." Elinor learned not to buy him clothes with designer labels because he wouldn't wear them. The family owned a Lexus for a time, but Eddie didn't like to drive it. When the architects for a new family home asked, "What would your husband like in the house design?" Elinor responded matter of factly, "He doesn't care." Eddie never even saw the plans.

For Eddie life is centered in one place: the family. "I always felt like he put me, the kids, and now the grandkids first," Elinor says. Each night when he walks in the door, his attention turns to the family. His pool play with his grandkids when they were toddlers included "dolphin tag," in which the person who is "it" must utilize only the dolphin kick. Pool games with "Papa" led Holly's son Luke to a college swimming career in the Longhorn class of '21.

*2010 Christmas ski trip with the grandkids*

Holly entered St. Edwards University in Austin, a Catholic school. She gradually became interested in Catholicism and was particularly fascinated by 1981 sightings of the Virgin Mary in Medjugorje, Bosnia and Herzogovina (then Yugoslavia). People who had witnessed the phenomenon were gathering at a conference in New Orleans to share their experiences. When their daughter wanted to go, Eddie and Elinor went with her.

The Reese women began discussing going to Medjugorje to see and visit with witnesses. Their thought, conversation, and prayer regarding the potential trip lasted many months. As the optimum time to plan for Holly's spring break approached, a normally protective Eddie surprised them by pointing out that if they wanted to go during spring break, they had better start planning.

Elinor had always wanted to travel, and one of the things she most appreciated about Eddie's success was that it gave them the means to do so. The coach's responsibilities for the collegiate season wouldn't permit him to make the trip, nor would Heather's college schedule, but off to Medjugorje went Elinor, Holly, and a friend.

Generally, thousands of visitors tour Medjugorje every day of

  Chuck Warner

the year. At that time, however, war had erupted nearby in Croatia. Against a backdrop of bombings in the distance, the ladies set aside their fears about the danger and were treated to a great adventure, visiting with people who had witnessed the sightings.

At about the same time, Elinor had begun spiritual exploration in other areas as well. In 1997 her fascination with the work of Mother Teresa led her and a friend to plan a trip to Calcutta to learn how to better contribute globally. Elinor only half-jokingly said, "It takes two weeks to make an appointment to see your local pastor, but we fly to Calcutta, and it took twenty-four hours."

In the sweltering July heat, Elinor and her friend landed in Calcutta. Their luggage had been lost and they were highly visible prey to potential swindlers. The two made their way to the chapel that hosted Mother Teresa's work. As there were no chairs, they knelt on a cloth laid out on a concrete floor, sweat pouring down their arms, and explained to the sisters that they were there to see Mother Teresa and volunteer for her work.

The excited sisters said that Mother Teresa was right across the road. The sisters then stopped six lanes of traffic to walk the exhausted visitors across the street. For the next two weeks the ladies from Austin woke at 5:30 a.m. and spent each long day assisting Mother Teresa at her House of the Dying and on the streets of Calcutta.

On the day they were flying back to Texas, Elinor offered the sisters some money to help support their work. They said, "No, give it to Mother."

Elinor tried. But the eighty-six-year-old nun looked Elinor square in the eyes and instructed her to "Go home and work with the poorest of the poor in Austin."

In the twenty years since her visit to Calcutta, that is what Elinor Reese has done, but now with an increased intensity to seek out people that need help. Her efforts have included finding the poorest neighborhoods in Austin and posting her phone number with a note: "Call me if you need help." She didn't even stop on the days she had committed to babysit Holly's son Reese; the toddler went along with Elinor, quickly becoming known by name to the homeless and needy in and around Austin.

Today Elinor's days continue to be filled with her jail ministry and work in shelters. She and Eddie have opened their home to people with mental and emotional problems, at times providing a house key so they could come and go as they pleased. They have even helped put some through college.

Kris Kubik explains, "There were days Eddie would walk into morning practice at 5:45 a.m., having just been with Elinor feeding the homeless under bridges in Austin. He would tell me, 'I can't believe the places we visited. I was scared for my life. I don't know how Elinor does it.'"

Who better to coach Eddie Reese than Elinor?

*Reese Mob, Costa Rica December 2017*

"Long ago, Elinor told Eddie to make sure he kept whatever commitments he makes," says Kubik. "That's not easy, because he gets so many requests that it's hard to fulfill all of them. He might, for

 Chuck Warner

example, have told the Kiwanis Club he would speak at their function and then wish he could go to the volleyball game instead. He can get very overscheduled, but with Elinor's initial encouragement, he has made a habit of keeping every commitment he makes."

**The tougher the battle (life), the
greater the gifts of rewards.**

*Elinor telling men's and women's team about her cancer diagnosis.*

At this writing, Elinor is dealing with "treatable cancer." The day she found out the news, Eddie came home and told her he was canceling a recruiting trip to Cincinnati. She said, "No, you're not."

Eddie pushed back. "Elinor, you have cancer."

Elinor would not be deterred. "Yes, and I will be here when you get back. You said you would go see the recruit. Go." And he did.

In a 2008 conversation at the American Swimming Coaches World Clinic, someone asked Eddie, "When are you going to retire from coaching?"

Before he could answer, Elinor jumped in with a smile. "When I tell you to." When he decided to continue after Kris Kubik stepped down after the 2016 Olympic Trials, Elinor said, "Then you'll have to coach through the 2020 Games."

Eddie may be everyone else's coach, but Elinor is his.

*Great Guana Cay, Abacos, Bahamas July 2013*

Together Elinor and Eddie have enjoyed many trips to the Olympics. But Elinor's favorite event is the NCAA Swimming Championships, because of the excitement of the team competition. Throughout Eddie's successful coaching career he has exhibited wit, warmth, and wisdom, but he also coaches young men with the perspective of seeing a slice of the world through Elinor's eyes and her extraordinary demonstrations of kindness. If you're patient enough to wait around until the completion of the UT team celebration at the NCAAs, you'll see Eddie and Elinor walking off the pool deck the way they both feel most happy: hand in hand.

Eddie and Elinor Reese's experiences have helped take them around the world. When asked what the highlight is for her, Elinor melts back into her chair as though her husband's arms are surrounding her and says, "My highlight is just being with Eddie."

**I wouldn't have accomplished
one-tenth of what I have in
my life without Elinor.**

# How Does Eddie Coach?

# Leadership

*Bear the pain.*

*Eddie and Mike McBroom*

THE WORD LEADERSHIP, ESPECIALLY IN COACHING, CAN bring to mind a commanding figure pushing the group forward. When we began working for Eddie in 1978 it quickly became apparent that he wasn't that type of leader. His combination of kindness, high moral character, and striving for excellence signaled team members and staff alike to find similar qualities in themselves. He models a standard and then constantly and selflessly coaches everyone around him to bring those qualities out in themselves.

In addition to his parents, Eddie had excellent role models when he was a child. Until he reached the age of twelve, he was an avid Little League baseball player. One day his father told him that their cousin, Snag Holmes, was coaching swimming and wondered if he might like to give it a try. Eddie was happy to comply, and younger brother Randy followed along.

Laughing, Eddie describes his initial miserable experience with swimming, "When my face was in the water, I was crying—crying in the water, but not out." Two months later he won the 50-meter butterfly at a state meet and became hooked on swimming.

Snag told Eddie, "Good swimmers don't drink alcohol." Eddie didn't, hasn't, and doesn't.

His dutiful attitude toward his coaches helped him become a high school state champion and record holder in the 200 individual medley. "The ten-and-under girls today could beat it," he quips.

At the University of Florida his leadership qualities gained recognition. He was elected team co-captain his senior year. When he returned to Gainesville after his stint in New Mexico, even as an assistant coach, he was integral to the team's coaching.

The main thing is to keep the main<br>thing the main thing.

Acting like a gentleman is an early lesson for every swimmer Eddie Reese has coached. Neil Caskey '12, team captain in 2012, explains:

> *At Texas we had a pool full of world-class, world-record holding, Olympic-gold-medal-winning athletes, but Eddie made sure that was no excuse to treat people poorly. If we went out to dinner as a team, we always went with the rule to leave the place cleaner than we found it and be the best customers they'd ever had. He taught us to be good people and treat people right, and he lived that every day.*

Terry Warner SMU '74 shares three examples as a coaching colleague:

> *When Eddie was looking for a home in Austin, I was down there visiting him. As I listened to him explain his requirements for the right home in this big family move, I had a lot of other possibilities running through my mind—two-car garage, fireplace, big yard, etc.—but Eddie's only consideration seemed to be wanting to be sure his bedroom was within view and listening distance of his two little girls, Holly and Heather.*
>
> *In 1982 I went to coach the University of North Carolina at*

*Charlotte. The next year I asked Eddie to come to Charlotte and give a clinic. I thought it would help bring more attention to our program and help the coaches in our area. Surely there would be great interest in learning from someone with a recent NCAA team title? He agreed and made the trip. Only about five coaches showed up for the clinic. I was embarrassed at the low turnout, but he stayed the entire day. A few days later he called me to make sure I was doing okay.*

*Our coach at SMU, George McMillion, was about ten years older than Eddie. They had their share of competitive battles over the years. When "Coach Mac" passed away in November of 2017, Eddie missed practice and traveled the 400 miles round-trip from Austin to Dallas with Kris Kubik for the funeral. Someone approached Eddie and tried to strike up a conversation pertaining to swimming. He said, "This isn't about swimming, it's about people."*

*George McMillion enrolled at SMU in 1950 and was a valued leader on campus for more than fifty years. As head coach, he guided SMU Men's Swimming & Diving from 1971 to 1988 and, for more than twenty additional years, continued to serve SMU.*

*Richard Quick shared the pool deck as the
Texas Women's coach 1982–88*

It is hard to imagine someone who loves the sport of swimming more than Eddie Reese. The late great Coach Richard Quick (six-time Olympic coach with thirteen NCAA team titles) once told a story about wanting to spend some time with Eddie. Richard said that although he hated fishing, he joined Eddie anyway to listen and learn. As Richard told it, Eddie went on and on about this guy and that guy on his team and how much faster they could swim. With a smile, Richard said, "I got sick of listening to it!!" Richard put up with the fishing to learn from Coach Reese, but one of the lessons was how much of Eddie's joy centers around his swimmers' going faster.

Eddie Reese's enthusiasm for engaging those around him in the process of swimming faster motivates nearly all his athletes.

　　　　Chuck Warner

Athletes who lose their passion for improving and can't rekindle it, even with the help of a coach, are probably not suitable for an Eddie Reese team. If a swimmer is all-in, Eddie's all-in. And whether you are an athlete or staff member of an Eddie Reese-coached team, his desire to support you on your life's journey knows no limit.

Longhorn 2012 team captain Hayes Johnson shares Eddie's impact on two of his college experiences:

*My freshman year, my parents told me they were getting a divorce. I held it in for far too long and it finally got to me one practice, causing me to get out and rush to the bathroom to hide my tears. (He could sense these kinds of things from a mile away.)*

*Eddie walked in along with two seniors on the team, grabbed my arm, and said, "Everything will be okay. We are your family." And I proceeded to get back to the pool deck to finish practice. I wasn't expecting anyone or anything to "come to the rescue" but, wow, that was nice to hear as an eighteen-year-old in a brand-new place and with my world turned upside down.*

Then:

*Fast forward to my senior year. I underwent a brutal eye surgery and knew that it was going to impact my final year as captain of the team. It was a terrible feeling walking into the pool the first time after surgery—wearing an eye patch and obnoxiously large sun glasses—knowing that I wasn't going to be in the water for the first time in four years with my brothers and teammates. I remember seeing Eddie ...*

*He waved me over, gave me the best hug in the world as I teared up, and said, "We are going to get you back, and you will qualify for NCAAs." It wasn't much, but the way he said it made me want to run through a wall.*

Making the sport of swimming one of the most successful and popular Olympic sports in America and the world requires a great deal of volunteer coach leadership. Eddie has contributed by serving on many committees in the NCAA, USA Swimming, and on the Board of Directors for the American Swimming Coaches Association. Not only has he contributed his own ideas to the programming and development of American and international swimming, he also supports others serving to improve the sport.

To appreciate the following anecdote, it's important to know a bit about its teller.

Coach Casey Converse was once a swimmer training under Coach Mark Schubert at Mission Viejo. During his high school years, Casey wasn't always on time (or at practice at all). Nevertheless, at Mission Viejo he worked hard, subsequently earning a spot on the 1976 USA Olympic team (Montreal).

Although Casey began his college education at Alabama—where he became the first human ever to swim faster than fifteen minutes in the 1650-yard freestyle (14:57.39)—it took some additional time to eventually earn his B.A. from Washburn University (Kansas) in 1984. Coach Casey Converse matured into a tremendous leader in his own right, eventually serving as head coach at the United States Air Force Academy from 1988 to 2017. During that time he also served on the NCAA Swimming Committee with Coach Reese.

Here is Casey's story:

*We were in a meeting room and it was adjourning. I got up, went down the hall to the elevator to go up to my room. I noticed someone hurrying to catch up to me. I look around—it's Eddie Reese. He says to me, "Casey, Mark Schubert would be so proud of you for your service on the committee."*

*How could someone who knew me so little care so much*

*to support me—and do it in such a meaningful way as to bring Mark into it to emphasize his point?*

Well into his tenure at Texas, Eddie recounted a story of how Elinor had suggested he read the book *Leadership Is an Art,* by Max DePree. He loved the book and took note of a passage that suggests a good leader "bears the pain of the group."

Coach George Block, a leader in international swimming as well as his San Antonio, Texas, community, shares this story:

*Post-retirement I was at the NCAAs giving a NISCA (National Interscholastic Swimming Coaches Association) talk. On the last day Eddie's team had "under-performed." (I think they were fifth or some number that would be a career highlight for the rest of us.) While most of them were still pretty pumped about their achievements, Eddie pulled the team over to a corner and essentially told them, "We can be much better than this and we WILL be much better than this. I knew this outcome was coming, and it is my fault that I didn't prepare you better. We will be better prepared. I am making changes, and those changes will start one week from Monday."*

*What a leadership lesson in the power of ownership. I guess the changes worked. He won the next three NCAA Championships.*

Coach Reese's leadership qualities include internal persistence in striving for excellence. And he has the confidence that over time, by doing the right thing, his athletes and teams will achieve it.

**Have patience or you become one.**

# Chapter 7

# Motivation

*I don't yell at them, I yell FOR them.*

One-on-one conversations with Eddie were rare during the short time I worked for him. A key one happened one day when I was riding with him in his car. We were driving south on I-35 when he graciously asked about my background as a swimmer. I remember telling him that, as impressive as his coaching was, I thought my old coach Jim Barton was the greatest motivating swim coach I had ever seen. Jim, who was once the freshman coach at Yale, would march the pool deck like a drill sergeant, controlling our efforts through his enthusiasm or his reprimands. In brief, we

　Chuck Warner

felt an external force of motivation from him. However, as a young coach and no longer an impressionable youth, I had a lot to learn about internal versus external motivation, especially as it pertains to coaching national and world class swimmers.

**Take it upon yourself to have the kind of year you dream about. Have a goal each day.**

The motivation of Eddie's swimmers comes primarily from their inner being; it is a force more powerful than any external source can deliver.

**One of the most important things DeLoss Dodds told me is that if you want someone to believe something, you tell them [they can do it] a lot.**



*A milestone by Townley Haas*

Eddie cultivates a partnership with each of his athletes that is founded upon a single mission—to discover how fast they might become. After the 2017 World Championships in Budapest he noted, for example, that any motivation for Olympic 100-meter butterfly champion Joseph Schooling would have to be internal. Joseph needed to decide if he was still passionate about improving and in turn willing to "work when it hurt" to continue to go faster. Schooling says, "Eddie was patient—very, very patient—with me. If he had forced me to come back, I would have probably refused. But he let me come back when I was ready—didn't push me at all." External sources could not motivate him consistently.

When I was in my mid-thirties, Coach Barton told me, "Coaching is a young man's game. At your age, you've got a little time left." Jim may have been right, if I were to coach with that daily overt passion that marched him up and down the pool deck. But Eddie Reese's style of connecting with and nurturing the dreams of his athletes has proven more effective and obviously far more enduring.

At Auburn Eddie took over as head coach of a team that hadn't scored a point at the 1972 NCAA Championship. The fledgling coach turned to coaches like Alabama's Don Gambril for answers to his hundreds of questions. Although young, Eddie did have strong ideas on how he would motivate his swimmers.

### I tried to say three to five nice things to each swimmer each day.

What followed from 1974 to 1978 was a progression at NCAAs from seventeenth to eighth, eighth, fifth, and second.

A unique chemistry in the pool at Texas enhances each swimmer's motivation. Just about all the swimmers on the Longhorn men's squad were the fastest swimmers on their club and/or high school team. Consequently most of them are accustomed to winning sets in practice. Corralling a collection of winners in the same training session can create a very competitive atmosphere.

### As hard as I ask them to go, they go harder.

Assistant coach Kris Kubik shares an example:

*It was early in Aaron Peirsol's freshman year. Eddie gave them a set of something like five rounds of 1 x 200-yard individual medley (IM) on 2:30, 300 freestyle on 3:30, 3 x 100s on 1:15. They were supposed to start with an easy 200 IM, then a fast 300 free, easy 100s, and then continue that pattern of alternating easy, fast swimming through the set.*

*Aaron blew everyone out of the pool with a 1:51 on the 200 IM to start the set. I walked over and said, "Aaron, do you know that one was supposed to be easy?"*

*Aaron said, "I know."*

With so many great athletes in the pool—dozens, over the years, that have won Olympic gold medals—infighting and intra-team rivalries could be common. Instead Coach Reese has created a culture in which teammates encourage teammates to get faster and winning is a lower priority.

Tate Jackson '19 told how he and Brett Ringold '18 challenged one another on a set of repeats:

*On Tuesdays we do 20 x 50s, leaving on three minutes (from a push off). Brett and I started out doing the first ten butterfly. After that we would get in a groove on freestyle. Brett started out with a 22.9. Then I went a 22.7. Brett said, "I can beat that," and went 21.7. I said, "easy-peasy" and went 21.4. Then I got Brett really angry by talking some smack, and he pushes a 20.4 and (smiling) ruins the game, because I'm not going faster than that [20.4]! Then we both died for a bit but then started bringing our times back down.*

Later in that 2018 season Tate Jackson set a new Texas school record in the 100-yard freestyle of 41.27.

**If you want to beat people you have to be willing
to do some things they're not willing to do.**

Before practice Eddie will talk with his team in an effort to teach "success habits" to help them improve in swimming and in life. His talks include reinforcing what his swimmers do well both out of the pool and in it, but when practice starts he expects self-motivated athletes in the pool. Clark Smith '17 explains Coach Reese's approach this way: "Eddie leaves the effort up to you. He provides a set, along with an explanation of how hard he wants you to go. You can choose not to work hard, not get better; Eddie may take the blame for it, but that falls on your shoulders."

*Aaron Peirsol, the greatest male backstroker in swimming history. Five-time Olympic Gold Medalist.*

Although champions like Aaron Peirsol are very self-motivated, Coach Reese still has a knack of deftly employing a challenge so subtle that it is almost subliminal, and it is very, very effective. This is one example from Aaron's freshman year at Texas:

(Excerpt from the book … *And Then They Won Gold*)

*By late January the team and Aaron were tired from hard training. They took the bus four hours up to Dallas to swim SMU in a tri-meet with Arizona. Aaron loved the experience of college swimming, the dual meets and the team camaraderie. But he also loved targets, goals and the thrill of achievements. When they arrived at the pool he stood under the pool record board and studied the times.*

*Eddie Reese walked up and stood next to him. "What are you looking at?"*

*Aaron answered, "the 1:43.8 200 back." Ryan Berube had set the pool record. He was the 1996 NCAA Swimmer of the Year and an Olympic Gold Medal winner. He was also a fantastic underwater dolphin kicker, making him a great short course swimmer.*

*Eddie told him, "You can't do that now [this time of the season]."*

*Aaron smiled, "I don't know about that."*

*When the 200-yard backstroke event came, Aaron ripped through the distance. As he approached the finish, he reached for the wall with his right hand and extended his left pinky and index finger into the "Hook 'em Horns" sign. He looked at the time on the board—1:42.8—and aimed the "Hook 'em Horns" gesture at Eddie and the team. Aaron Peirsol was officially a Texas Longhorn.*

Another example from John Martens:

*During winter break Eddie would bring the team to Salt Lick BBQ and then have them attempt to swim 20 x 50s fly on :35 the next morning … yes, even the sprinters. Character and team building after being stuffed with all-you-can-eat barbecue. Being a distance IM/fly swimmer, I had done 20 my freshman year, so this year he boasts to me that "he had a guy" that got up to 30. So I ended up making 44 x 50s on :35 to break that. He just smiles at me like he planned the whole thing from the beginning.*

Even for world class athletes like those on Coach Reese's teams, motivation can wane when individuals deal with other life issues. From Hans Dersch '90:

*Not many people know this, but the night before I was to leave Austin for the Olympic Trials in 1992, my brother called. "After you're done with your swim meet, come back to Atlanta. Mom has a brain tumor, and she might die."*

*I was so shaken by the news that my focus on the meet evaporated. The next day in Indy I was still in a fog. Swimming seemed trivial and unimportant. Doug Gjertsen, my roommate, learned what was happening and said, "You need to tell Eddie."*

*That night I told Eddie the news. He paused, absorbing it for a moment, then gently posed the perfect question: "Do you think your Mom would feel better if you gave up on this dream you've been working so hard on, or if you went out and did your best?"*

*I felt a huge weight lift off me, because of course he was right. The best thing I could do for my Mom was to do my best.*

*Eddie and Kris both taught that lesson regularly: Great coaching often has nothing to do with swimming.*

*The rest of the story is that Mom made it through two tough surgeries and is still doing well today, and Doug and I both made that 1992 Olympic team.*

**I see them going fast, then I see them believing it. And then I see them having to do it again, to believe it again.**

 Chuck Warner

This story about Olympian Ricky Berens appeared in the January 1, 2018, issue of *The Alcalde*:

> *At the 2008 Olympics in Beijing, Ricky Berens swam in the preliminary heat of the 4 x 200-meter freestyle relay, beating former 2000 and 2004 medalist Klete Keller by just four-tenths of a second, with head US men's swimming team coach Reese watching. As a rookie, Berens figured the veteran Keller would get the nod for the finals the next morning. After all, Keller had been there before, and Reese had been his coach in past Olympics. Headed to the warm-down pool after prelims, Berens figured he was done for the event.*
>
> *Ricky said: "Eddie walked up to me and said, 'I told the [other] coaches, "He's my swimmer, I got a lot of support for him." Get ready for tomorrow.'"*
>
> *Swimming the third leg of the relay, Berens, along with Michael Phelps, Ryan Lochte, and Peter Vanderkaay, took home the gold, setting a world record in the process.*
>
> *"That's when it matters most," Berens says, choking up. "He had my back. I still get teary-eyed thinking about it."*

Although many world class swimmers have stayed at Texas beyond their undergraduate years to train and pursue their dreams, Eddie knows that occasionally it's necessary to say goodbye.

> **When you get a shiny new car, you treat it wonderfully. Sometimes you can get to the point where that appreciation wears out.**

(Excerpt from the book ... *And Then They Won Gold*)

> *Coach Reese had said, "There are some swimmers where you earn your income coaching because they are challenging. Josh Davis is special. I would coach him for free." But the relationship had become too comfortable to bring out the best in Josh. Eddie believed in "shocking the body" with different*

*kinds of work in practices during each season and even from one season to the next. What happened next shocked Josh.*

*Eddie called Josh into his office. He knew a change was necessary in order for Josh to meet his potential and help the United States Olympic Team in 2000.*

*"Josh, my brother Randy is moving to Austin in January. I think you should go swim for him."*

*Josh couldn't believe what he was hearing. Leave Eddie? Leave Kris? Leave The University of Texas brethren he trained with? … He was more than shocked: he was stunned. But he knew in his heart that, as usual, Eddie was right.*

At the 2000 Olympic Trials Josh Davis broke Matt Biondi's twelve-year-old American Record in the 200-meter freestyle. At the Olympics in Sydney he swam even faster.

*Josh Davis 2000 American Record*

Over time a swimmer's motivation progresses from swimming for mom and dad when they are young to for their coach as they

 Chuck Warner

get older. Ultimately swimmers come closest to achieving their potential when they develop an internal motivation for reaching it, even if that potential is years away. Patience and persistence and the ability to delay gratification for their racing performance for many months are some of the characteristics that make swimmers some of the most unique athletes in the world.

Lydia Chase '93 remembers a training trip (with the men's and women's teams) to the Olympic Training Center in 1990. Eddie was delivering an inspirational speech before the difficult practice to follow. He emphasized the athlete's commitment to the hard, consistent work necessary to achieve one's swimming goals. He used one of his favorite statements, and Lydia has always remembered it:

**This sport chooses you, you don't choose it.**

# CHAPTER 8

# Strength

*If I can plug a swimmer into an outlet, measure their strength, and it increases when we plug them in again, then I think I have a faster swimmer.*

MANY CONSIDER FLEXIBILITY AND SUPPLENESS THE KEY physical attributes of a potentially elite swimmer. Long ago Eddie Reese recognized that the athlete's capacity for strength is also important.

A seminal moment in Eddie's burgeoning coaching career occurred when he was in grad school at the University of Florida. A classmate approached him and asked, "Why do swimmers try to get their strength in the water rather than out of it?" Eddie's personal swimming career had recently come to an end, but he began to consider the possibilities for helping his swimmers improve their strength out of the water.

The quote at the top was a declaration by Coach Reese in the 1970s. He was reflecting on developing his swimmers' strength with heavy weights, standard free weights exercises such as squats, bench press, weighted dips, etc. When he fully applied this approach in



Chuck Warner

his first head coaching stint at Auburn, the improvement in his swimmers was nothing short of stunning.

As with all his coaching, Eddie's view of developing a swimmer's strength has evolved, grown, and improved over time. But he has always held the belief that if a swimmer low in body mass can effectively apply pressure on the water—or has great distance per stroke—then gains in strength to increase that pressure will accelerate their improvement.

In his first year as an assistant coach at Texas (1978), Dana Abbott had this experience:

> *I spent my first few days with freshman Louis Mestier, one of my club swimmers from Mississippi and a backstroker in whom Eddie had shown an interest. We were exploring the UT campus and wound up in the athletic offices at Memorial Stadium. As we came out of the athletic office reception area, there was Eddie Reese. I introduced Louis, and Eddie said, "So you're the one with eighteen-inch biceps—nine inches on your left arm and nine inches on your right."*
>
> *The three of us had a good laugh. In that moment, though, Eddie sent a few messages to Louis. He cared enough about him to know his background, that he already had considered how to help Louis get faster, and that his experience at Texas would likely be fun.*

**My guys have to take their rings off to perform curls.**

Robert Bogart '98 quickly learned that getting stronger would be important during his recruiting trip to Texas:

> *I was at a BBQ restaurant with Eddie and Elinor. Both Eddie and I had finished our plates while Elinor was still eating. He looked over at her and pointed to the chicken breast still on her plate and asked, "Are you going to eat that?" She replied "No, I'm getting full." He took what was left on her plate, dumped it on to mine, and said, "You need to gain at least ten pounds."*

Not every incoming freshman is as skinny as Robert was, but Eddie's ability to design an individualized program to develop strength in each of his swimmers has been his forte. The most ideal body is one in which the addition of a little muscle bulk will not hinder the athlete's ability to split through the water. For example, when world recorder Aaron Peirsol committed to Texas, although Eddie claimed to be nervous about coaching such an accomplished swimmer he also confided, "but he has no body."

**You can hold him to a light and see his bone
structure, literally. And all we have been
trying to do is get him to gain weight.**

That quote isn't specifically in reference to Aaron, but it does properly characterize many of Eddie's freshmen over the years. The coach's education helped him appreciate the importance of researching and testing his athletes. The vertical jump test had been a regular test of explosive ability in his program.

**In a vertical jump contest between him
and a dead man, he'd get second.**

Eddie likes to introduce something new each year. Sometimes it's an exercise. In the fall of 1978 one of those new things was "vertical sit-ups." He had straps stitched together with one loop at one end and two loops at the other. We used the single loop to hang them off the balcony railing at the north end of the pool. With the help of a teammate, swimmers could put their feet into the two dangling loops, hang vertically, and perform sit-ups. A key to effectively developing abdominal muscle strength was to have a teammate or coach help the swimmer keep from swinging and perform each sit-up with control.

The exercise had an element of risk to it, because the athlete hung upside down. It was minimized, to some degree, by having the head lowered to just a few inches from a mat placed on the tiled pool deck. American record holder Scott Spann was about 6'2" tall and very strong. One day as Scott was doing sit-ups his strap broke as his head neared the floor. Then again on another day. We stopped doing vertical sit-ups.

Today Scott has earned the title "Dr. Spann" and is an orthopedic surgeon living in Austin. So, it seems, everything turned out fine.

### Was he flexing? How could you tell?

Eddie's strength development program generally consists of two parts: weightlifting on Mondays, Wednesdays, and Fridays, and dryland exercises on Tuesdays and Thursdays that could include box jumps, rope climbing, crawling in a prone position on "wheels" (lawn mower wheels attached to the ends of a short piece of padded 2x4), and doing sit-ups while strapped to surgical tubing (to keep tension on the upper body). The key to his program and the development of a swimmer's strength is progression. In other words, the goal isn't for everyone to go into the weight room to lift a set amount of weight. Instead, Eddie strives to help each athlete increase personal strength while maintaining the shoulder mobility necessary for proper streamlining and avoiding an increase in non-productive bulk.

Before his freshmen went into the weight room in 2016 Eddie told them a story about a swimmer who was only bench pressing 135 pounds. When he saw Brendan Hansen doing 250 pounds on bench press for ten repetitions, he improved his bench press up to 165 pounds for ten reps and won NCAAs only a few tenths slower than Brendan.

When asked once what he does to motivate his swimmers in the weight room, Eddie replied:

### I unlock the doors.

To help his freshman adapt to his strength program, Eddie's approach has evolved so that now during their initial fall semester he tests them every third week. For example, by comparing bench-press sets—such as a set of 6-4-2 repetitions—he can receive numerical feedback on the first-year swimmer's progress or lack thereof. He will often give freshmen a week or two off weights in late November, enabling them to adapt to their workload, in preparation for swimming fast at an early December invitational.

In his own words:

**If somebody has been in my program two or three years and a freshman comes in and I have got the freshman doing the same thing that guy is doing, I'm not very smart. Because that freshman cannot do that, if I run a good program and make it harder every year.**

---

 Chuck Warner

# CHAPTER 9

# Technique

*Stroke work is like yardwork or housework. If you do not keep up with it, it just gets so bad.*

Kris Kubik says, "Eddie is a genius at stroke technique." In the same way that a race car driver uses his skill to race a finely engineered automobile, technique is the skill that allows the swimmer to race his or her body/machine as fast as possible.

Not far from his boyhood home in Daytona Beach was Marineland, the forerunner to Sea World. When Eddie was a child he loved to visit and watch the movement, flow, and speed of fish as they weaved through the water. This was the foundation to developing his understanding of how a swimmer could travel underwater, accelerate through breakouts, employ efficient technique, and more.

*Eddie Reese's idea for studying fish and underwater dolphin kicking.*

**You've got to be careful because some real
good swimmers can make a stroke work that
won't work for most of us normal humans.**

When he was growing up, Eddie had heard about the "bent arm backstroke." He and his friends began experimenting with a recovery that imitated freestyle, with the elbow bent upon the entry. Then they learned that the "bent arm" referred to the pull *underwater*. This was an early lesson on configuring stroke technique on sound principles of physics, not on what you hear, and not even what you might see a fast swimmer do. As Coach Reese likes to say, "It may be the only thing that's hurting him/her."

**Don't put a limit on stroke technique
or how fast you can go.**

With a discerning eye, Eddie will watch the fastest swimmers at top-level competitions and then adopt for his swimmers only the elements that he judges meet sound physical principles and promote effective movement through water. From childhood to the present, watching fish and dolphin undulations, sculling, sweeping, and various other forms of movement through water has developed Eddie's meticulous art of discerning the elements of swimming fast.

**There are no little mistakes.**

Coach Reese's teams concentrate on refining the little things—the details. Because Eddie has such a keen eye for the minute details of a start, a turn, or a technique, he can address it with clarity and decisiveness with his athletes. He often has his team members pair up and coach one another. One swimmer will stand on the deck watching their partner's starts or turns. "It's very humbling to watch them listen to each other more than they listen to me."

*Kip Darmody and Tripp Cooper*

**This meet [NCAAs] is being decided by five
feet over three days. You've got to be 3.5
feet on the right side of that five feet.**

When I worked at Texas (1978–79), the team practiced turns
three to four times each week for ten to fifteen minutes, typically
on the days we had a little extra time at the end of practice. This
concentrated period enabled each swimmer to swim straight in
and straight out from the wall, rather than the "circle swimming"
they had done throughout practice.

One day Eddie said to me, "Let's watch some [freestyle]
turns." We sat on the starting blocks watching the guys perform
freestyle turns. He explained the leg positioning he was looking
for and how to achieve a straight push-off rather than applying a
downward force that creates an ineffectual angle when bouncing
off the wall.

I tried again and again but I couldn't see what he saw. Eventually I grasped the ninety-degree knee position (when the point
of the feet contact the wall) and the body's straight line on the
push off the wall that he wanted. As he helped me train my focus
I could see it, it clicked, and it stuck. Eddie doesn't just coach
the swimmers. He coaches the coaches, too.

**Going faster isn't just moving the arms and legs faster.**

One of the great realizations for any experienced coach is that
poor technique dramatically decreases an individual's chance of
competing at a high level—like trying to race a poorly streamlined car. The harder the engine works, the more the resistance
of the car works against itself. Of course, excellent stroke technique *increases* the probability of effectiveness and reaching
the individual's ultimate potential. Effective stroke technique
is generally centered on how much distance the swimmer can
travel with each stroke cycle.

 Chuck Warner

**Coaches can't make stroke changes; the
swimmer has to decide to make them.**

## FREESTYLE

**The best entry anybody on your team makes
is when they reach [their hand] for the wall, as
they finish. So we teach "reach for the wall."**

When we were first assisting at Texas, many of the athletes needed significant technical improvement to realize their potential. The late Bernie Kissel was one of those. He was tall, had a good swimmer's physique, and was willing to work. Bernie had a habit of bending his wrist on his entry, thus his hand, wrist, and forearm didn't cut cleanly through the surface of the water.

One day Eddie said to us, "I'll give a nickel to anyone that can fix Bernie's freestyle." We all worked like heck to help Bernie, to have Eddie recognize our contribution, and to earn that nickel.

Bernie's freestyle entry improved but didn't become perfect. A lot of technical habits are firmly ingrained and hard to change by the time swimmers get to college.

**If straight arm [recovery] is good at the end
of a race, why not use it the entire race?**

Eddie Reese Tips:
- Recover your arm with a high-elbow.
- Water level is in the middle of the crown of the head.
- Enter as though you're finishing your last stroke.
- Pull with the fingers pointed toward the bottom as much as possible.
- Keep the elbow higher than the hand.
- Put the head directly back in line with the body after a breath.

The best swimmers usually initiate a "grip" on the water by creating a vertical forearm out in front of their shoulder and under the chest. Recently Eddie pointed out that today's technical understanding has the arm more extended than it was decades ago. And speed in all distances is increasing, as many swimmers—even those who are distance-oriented—tend to pull with their fingertips pointed toward the bottom, rather than to the side of the pool.

**The best kickers tend to be the best freestylers.**

To reach one's potential, improving the kick is essential.

*John Shebat backstroke start*

## BACKSTROKE

**Other strokes have variations, but there
is only one way to swim backstroke.**

                    Chuck Warner

Coach Reese Tips:

- While the eyes focus on the ceiling (straight up), the shoulders rotate "like they're on a barbecue skewer," running longitudinally through the center of the body.
- The hands enter at eleven and one o'clock, relative to the center line of the body.
- The pinky finger cuts into the water like you're cutting through butter with no mess.
- The hands start slow, accelerate through the pull, and finish fast, recovering quickly.

**The strongest and fastest backstrokers have the hand [pulling] further out from the body.**

In the 1960s the great Doc Counsilman conducted research measuring the angle of the forearm to the swimmer's upper arm, at the break of the elbow, during the backstroke pull. Many top swimmers were measured at about ninety degrees. Eddie utilizes the principle, "the longer the lever the more pressure on the water." Today Doc's research might show a 120-degree angle for some of the top backstrokers in the world. The increases in strength and physical size of today's swimmers allows the arm to be "longer," thereby exerting more pressure on the water (i.e., swimming faster).

**The finish of the stroke has become _boom!_, and the hand is gone.**

The finish of the stroke in backstroke is like a basketball free-throw follow-through. The snap of the wrist as the last bit of push is applied to the water is similar to the moment of release of the basketball. However, in contrast to a free throw, the hand "bounces" up from underwater into the air.

**In breaststroke, you can't swim all out to swim all out.**

Eddie's point is that the swimmer must wait for the feet to finish together before the hands begin the outsweep of the pull. Therefore, a streamline position should always be achieved, even momentarily, after the finish of the kick and before the initiation of the pull. (A poor kicker will begin the pull more quickly.) He notes that breaststroke is the hardest stroke to train, because it creates the most resistance.

**It's the hardest stroke to decide
what's best for the swimmer.**

Coach Reese Tips:
- Start and finish each stroke looking at the bottom of the pool in a full streamline.
- Watch what the hands do. They can get in the way (unless you circle them forward).
- Wait for your feet to touch prior to pressing the hands outward to begin each stroke.
- Your glide time depends on how strong your kick is.
- When your head is out of the water for a breath, look at the end of the pool.

**When your arms can't move in breaststroke,
your legs are going to go soon.**

Eddie believes in strengthening the arms and upper body by training *them*, not just the legs. Balancing the development of the arms and legs, as well as extending into a drive or glide at the end of each stroke, enables the swimmer to best utilize energy and swim faster. Eddie says the biggest mistake a breaststroker can make is collapsing the elbows into the ribs, as opposed to circling the hands forward into a streamline.

**It's a very simple stroke because you can only do
certain things that make it work properly.**

Coach Reese Tips:

- Hands enter at shoulder width.
- The breath is taken on alternate strokes, with the chin on the surface.
- The most important thing to look for is what the hips are doing.
- The hips rise as the feet go down.
- The hands snap through.

**If you can't kick fly, you can't swim fly.**

In the late 1980s and early 1990s underwater dolphin kicking was beginning to explode as a means of achieving speed. Eddie Reese quickly named it "the fifth stroke." When FINA (Fédération Internationale de Natation) changed the rules to allow a dolphin kick on the start and turn in breaststroke, the fifth stroke became a weapon in every stroke.

In the summer of 2016 UT's Joseph Schooling '18 kicked 10 x 100s long course on 1:40 with the first five times descending from 1:19 to 1:12 and the second five from 1:08 to 1:02. Schooling's superb fly kick helped him win the 2016 Olympic gold medal for 100 meters, defeating the great Michael Phelps.

**The best way for younger kids to learn fly kick
is on their backs with the hands at the side.**

Coach Reese likes developing the fly kick in this fashion because it allows the full head-to-toes body to engage in the dolphin motion. If the arms are placed over the head in a configuration approaching streamline, the axis of the body is longer, undulation decreases, and there is less "flow" through the shoulders to the toes. When pushing off a wall he tells his swimmers to take their first dolphin kick after they have traveled one body length, to avoid disrupting the streamline for the first kick.

**If you feel your feet kick on [the top of]
the water, you're kicking too big.**

During the 2015 season, after warmup at each morning workout, the team started practice with a set of dolphin kicks. At the NCAA Championships, an unprecedented six Longhorn swimmers qualified in the top eight for the finals of the 100 butterfly.



**When they flashed on the scoreboard six of
the top eight, my heart rate got over fifty.**

---

# Chapter 10

# Kris Kubik

*Kris is a genius at people.*

Coach Reese would be the first to say that the "secret bullet" to the care and training of thirty to forty male swimmers on the Longhorn team for thirty-five years has been assistant coach Kris Kubik. His impact has been a key to the success of the UT swimming program.

Organizing and administrating an NCAA Division I program that includes a rule book of approximately 400 pages is a large, complex undertaking. The responsibilities include arranging travel, scheduling facilities, helping athletes manage their academic schedule while representing their university athletically, evaluating prospective student-athletes, visiting them, hosting them, and more. In order to concentrate on coaching his swimmers, the head coach must have all these tasks covered in advance.

Kris was a critical contributor in all of these areas until his retirement in 2016. The honors that have recently been bestowed upon Kris would be the pinnacle of any coach's career but are particularly rare for an assistant coach. He has been named to the Texas Longhorn Hall of Honor, to the Texas Swimming & Diving Hall of Fame, and as a special assistant coach to the United States Olympic Team (2008).

**Every once in a while, we come across someone in our sport who is just a prodigy at anything and everything he does. Kris is one of those guys. He's a genius from knowing how to fix anything that goes wrong, including me.**

Kris grew up in Tennessee, where, at a young age, he discovered he could swim very fast. At just eight years old he swam a 25-yard backstroke in 15.6 seconds. One would have to search through thousands of eight-year-olds to find one that swims that fast free-style, but to do it backstroke is virtually unheard of. A myth? I wondered. But then Kris pulled up a picture on his cell phone of the club record board with his standing record from 1964. More than just talented, Kris was a student of the sport. He often fell asleep in his swim suit while reading Swimming World Magazine and in the morning continued reading where he had left off the previous night.

Kris' exceptional swimming talent is matched only by his desire to treat people fairly and with kindness. Once as a boy he noticed that some African-Americans were not permitted at the church his family was attending. He asked his mom, "Why would I want to go to a church that will not allow that family to attend?" His mother respected his concern, and Kris ceased attending that church for a time.

As he matured in the sport, Kris became a world class back-stroker. He competed in the 1972 USA Olympic Trials and in 1973 was ranked in the top twenty-five in the world in the 100-meter backstroke. As a high school senior he was recruited by Coach Reese to Auburn. Instead he chose North Carolina State University and swam under the tutelage of Coach Don Easterling.

Don was very effective at helping his swimmers become fast, but he was also a very, very tough coach. For example, when his prodigy,

Doug Russell, upset Mark Spitz in the 100-meter butterfly to win the gold medal at the 1968 Mexico City Olympics, Russell walked to the award podium wondering if his coach would acknowledge it with the rare praise that Doug yearned for.

Unfortunately, the Kubik-Easterling combination wasn't a good match for Kris, just as it wasn't for some other teammates. Scott Hammond was one of only three of the eighteen freshmen in his recruiting class that remained on the team all four years. Kris left NC State after one year and went home to Memphis, where he swam for the summer with Memphis State Swim Club and Dick Fadgen. After continuing to swim through most of that fall semester he decided to stop.

In 1977 Kris had unceremoniously ended what was once a very promising swimming career and was working toward his degree while living with his family. One day he received a phone call from Eddie Reese. Coach Reese wanted Kris's character and athletic evaluation of a swimmer in his area named Phil Nenon. As the conversation progressed, Eddie asked Kris what he was going to do for the rest of his life. Kris said, "I'm not sure."

Eddie explained, "It seems to me you'd be good at coaching. After all, you laughed at my jokes when I was recruiting you. And you enjoy talking with people."

Eddie offered Kris a spot as a volunteer coach at Auburn. Kris asked, "How much does that pay?"

Kris spoke with his parents about the offer. They felt that, given the way his swimming career had ended, a year of coaching while he completed his degree might help him leave the sport feeling better about it. They supported his decision to join Eddie at Auburn as a volunteer assistant coach.

During that first season (1977–78) Kris connected quickly with Eddie, who shared both his values and the knowledge of what his swimmers needed to reach their full swimming potential.

One of the things that surprised Kris, however, was the lengthy taper periods (weeks of sharpening prior to peak performance)

Eddie prescribed for his swimmers. As Kris remembers it, during six to seven weeks of taper, many days of each week might consist of warmup (Eddie's favorite: 500 swim, 400IM stroke drill, 300 kick, 200 of 4 x 50s IM, 100 easy, or called a "5-4-3-2-1"), followed by a couple of timed 50s.

Kris finally said to Eddie, "They're not going to [have enough endurance to] be able to last a fifty, let alone a hundred."

Two weeks prior to the SEC Championships there was an invitational at the University of Georgia that served as the "shave and taper" meet for those athletes that were not selected for the eighteen-member conference squad. Kris took the group to Georgia a couple of days prior to the arrival of those selected for the conference squad, to give them time to relax and focus on their upcoming performances. He noticed that a billboard outside the front entrance of the hotel held announcements, such as welcome messages for arriving groups. Kris asked the manager if he could have something posted on the sign.

When the Auburn conference squad pulled into the hotel parking lot on the team bus, the billboard read "5-4-3-2-1." The team had a great laugh, and Eddie Reese knew he had a creative, supportive assistant coach.

Two weeks later the team delivered a tremendous performance at the SEC Championships. And after another three weeks, Auburn finished in second place at the NCAA Championships, putting Kris' doubts over a long taper to rest.

When Eddie decided to move to Austin, Kris moved with him. Scott Hammond, then an aspiring young coach, also headed to Austin to learn from Coach Reese. Since Kris would be in Austin during the summer to help with the opening of the Longhorn Swim Camp, he offered to find housing for both assistant coaches.

Coach Hammond found, however, that Kris's real-estate hunting skills needed work. He recalls:

*Kris calls to tell me about this great deal on a three-bedroom house. He had done a search and found it on East 56 Street*

                    Chuck Warner

*in Austin. I couldn't believe the deal. Kris said he drove by and peeked in the windows. It looked amazing, and the two of us agreed to sign a one year lease. When it came time to move in we learned that the streets in Austin sometimes had "½ streets" between the primary streets, and the house Kris had "checked out" was the wrong one. A tree limb covered a sign that said East 55½ Street, so it was hardly visible from the street, which meant the house we rented was actually one more block over … For that year, we lived in the most atrocious place I've ever lived in my life. We learned the lesson about doing a walk-through before signing a lease!*

*Sam Kendricks announcing at NCAAs*

Sam Kendricks, now America's most prominent competitive swimming announcer, met Kris that summer at the first Longhorn Swim Camp. Sam was growing up in Irving, Texas, at the time. He explains:

*Even though Irving wasn't known for swimming, I decided to give up football to concentrate on the sport. In the spring*

*of 1977, I was a high school junior and my mother heard
about the Longhorn Swim Camp. She couldn't afford to send
me, but our team was having a "Swim-a-Thon" (fundraiser).
My mom and I talked about me earning enough money to go
to the camp. My mom was a smoker but she said she would
even swim with me. My mom and I easily earned the most
money on our Swim-a-Thon that year, and I earned enough
for the camp.*

*I walked into registration, and there was Eddie Reese. "So
you're from Irving, Texas? They roll up the sidewalks about
9:00 there, don't they?" I thought to myself "Who is this cat?"
But a few minutes later, I heard a gentler voice. Kris Kubik
introduced himself to me. "I just got in from Auburn a few
hours ago myself, Sam." I felt an immediate connection to Kris.*

In 1982 Kris decided to pursue a career in selling pharmaceuticals
to veterinarians. He quickly realized that he didn't want to make
a career out of driving around Arkansas trying to convince vets
to buy his brand. Just as his father had once coached high school
basketball but had later chosen to be a dentist, in part to provide
for his family, Kris was torn between the idea of supporting his
family and doing what he enjoyed.

When he met his wife, then April Russell, he told her dad,
David Russell (UT football player '59–'61), "I'm thinking of going
back to coaching but want you to know that I will take care of
your daughter."

David, who was a doctor, said, "The people that I know who
have had the greatest impact on people have been coaches."

It wasn't long before Kris returned to coach in Austin for the
Longhorn Aquatic Club. When Texas assistant coach and former
swim star Kris Kirchner took the head coaching position at South
Carolina, the assistant position re-opened. It was September and
Eddie called Kris to see about his interest.

Kris jumped at the chance to resume his role but did caution

                    Chuck Warner

Eddie, "I'm not twenty-three anymore. I'd like to be able to tell you what I think, even if I disagree with you. But I will always do it behind closed doors."

Eddie said, "I would welcome that."

*Kris and April Russell Kubik*

Kris continued in his role at Texas for thirty-five years, the same length of time his mother had worked at a university. *Why remain an assistant coach so long?* Kris just wasn't compelled to compete as a head coach. He loved his life working with Eddie and at UT.

"Why try to be happier than happy?" he says, looking back. "I surely would not have done it all these years next to him or alongside of him had it not been something that was uniquely special. I truly have always appreciated when our swimmers are interviewed and they say, 'Eddie and Kris.' That's really important to me."

Over his years at Texas, Kris was also a mainstay at the Longhorn Swim Camp, inspiring tens of thousands of younger swimmers like Sam Kendricks.

**He makes sure I make the right decisions. It would have been a challenge without him, and fortunately, I never had to find that out.**

At the 2004 Olympics it was common to see Texas swimmers on the awards podium. One alum noticed that the Texas swimmers had their hands over their hearts during the national anthem. He called Kris to tell him how proud he was to see the respect Texas swimmers habitually demonstrated.

That fall one of the UT swimmers questioned the team tradition of wearing a coat and tie on their day trips to competitions. Eddie asked Kris what he thought of making a change. Kris relayed the story about the alum's pride about how the Texas swimmers handled themselves in Athens. Eddie went into the team locker room and, with unaccustomed emotion in his voice, told his guys, "We have always worn coat and ties, and we will continue to, as long as I'm here."

Like Eddie, Kris saw the value in each squad member. "People will look at who won an Olympic gold medal or who broke a world record. They won't necessarily know who came in at fifty-one seconds in the 100 butterfly and dropped down to forty-eight seconds and how much that meant to the team, or when there were other people who came in at a forty-eight and dropped down to a forty-five. Sometimes the kid who goes from fifty-one to forty-eight inspired the one to go from forty-eight to forty-five. That's special."

A former swimmer explained the relationship between Eddie and Kris this way: "Kris and Eddie have a dynamic. Eddie is visionary and Kris is the memory, practice, and action-oriented man

 Chuck Warner

behind the scenes. Kris has a gift of seeing patterns and relating people to the tradition that has come before them."

*Coach Kubik and Coach Reese 1987 NCAAs*

While Eddie Reese designed training, Kris was constantly searching for ways to make a positive difference for the athletes on the team, as well as others he touched in his life.

(Excerpt from the book … *And Then They Won Gold*)

*In 1995, Josh Davis was recently married and struggling to support his new family while training toward the 1996 Olympics. Davis swam the fastest 200-meter freestyle of any American in the summer of '95 but performed the time leading off a relay. This didn't fulfill the USA federation guidelines for funding athletes for the forthcoming Olympic year. Kris sent a fax to the USA Swimming National Team Director's office with a headline, "#1 Swimmer In the World Can't Afford a Meal." In Kris's letter he said "that while the USA National Resident Team is presently staying in a five-star hotel in Hawaii, Josh can't afford an eight pack of hot dogs." Josh received the funding and went on to win three gold medals at the 1996 Olympics in Atlanta—the most of any male athlete at those Games.*

Swimmers tell how Kris made a difference in their swimming in ways that went beyond their training.

Three-time Olympian Brendan Hansen '04 shared this:

*I remember getting ready for an Olympic finals of the 100 breaststroke. Kris gave me a picture of myself he found some-where, where I'm flexing my muscles. I was probably seven years old. He gave it to me and underneath it, it said, "This kid has always dreamed of winning a gold medal!" You get so wrapped up in a pressure-packed situation, and a moment like that brings it all back into perspective. He keeps you grounded and puts life first. His point was, "You're still that little kid. Just go have fun and enjoy yourself."*

**He's just a good friend who looks out for me. He knows when I need to be sent home or when I need something special. He reads everybody like that, and he is real good at it.**

Kris was so good at what he did that in 2007 he was named to the USA coaching staff for the Pan American Games, in 2008 made a special assistant to the national team director on the Olympic staff, and in 2009 served as USA coach on the World Championship in Rome.

From Olympic gold medalist Garrett Weber-Gale '07:

*In 2004 I missed making the US Olympic team by one spot,*

   Chuck Warner

*and I was so devastated. I didn't know what to do. I was bawling my eyes out, and it was the biggest disappointment to me. Kris talked to me afterward, and he was the perfect guy with words. The scoreboard was still showing the results from the 100 free finals. He said, "Remember this feeling right now and promise yourself you won't let yourself have this pain and disappointment ever again." He helped me get through that a lot. Over the next four years, people like Kris and Eddie Reese were so positive.*

Kris decided to retire from coaching after the 2016 Olympic Trials. Eddie Reese tried to explain the impact. "I talked to the team about that after he left. 'We're all going to have to help fill the void. You're going to have to help me take care of people. If someone needs a lot of help, get me. If they need help from someone on the team, give them that help.'"

**We were lucky to have [Kris] in the sport
and for me as a friend for lots of years.**

The symbiotic relationship between Coach Reese and Coach Kubik can't be overstated. Their mutual affection for people and sincere desire to make a difference in the lives of others for four decades has been like a finely choreographed Broadway production. If Eddie saw the big picture, Kris choreographed it.

One of many examples is the story conveyed earlier by Terry Warner about Eddie and Kris attending SMU Coach George McMillion's memorial service. Kris was actually in Dallas and called Eddie: "Coach Mac's memorial service is the day after tomorrow at one. There is a flight out of Austin that will get you there in time. I'll pick you up at the airport, we can attend the service, and I'll have you back on the five o'clock flight. How about we go?"

Eddie: "You bet."

*Kris Kubik starts a tradition of drying the
starting block for a Texas relay.*

Like a great basketball player that shares the ball, Kris made others around him better. When Kris stepped down as assistant coach he offered these thoughts: "I hope when people reflect back on Kris Kubik, they would say quite simply that he cared and it showed. I don't know if I always did the right thing for people, but I tried to. I always listened to my heart and strived to do what was best for each swimmer and diver."

**There is no chance of ever replacing
Kris, and we will miss him dearly.**

"I truly have never looked at Eddie as a boss," Kubik said. "I've looked him straight in the eye as a dear friend … He made every single day an adventure."

In 2018 Kris was inducted into the Texas Swimming & Diving Hall of Fame. Former swimmers and a few colleagues and friends were asked to contribute a one-word description of Kris for the occasion. They were:

　　　　　　　　Chuck Warner

Caring—Elinor Reese

Enthusiast—Pat Patterson

Respectful—Darrell Fick

Passionate—Ted Doyle & Kevin McKenna

Mentor—Scott Mactier

Glue—holds the team together—Mike Brown

Glue—Jim Henry

Selfless—Chris Plonsky

Treasure (as in he has a treasure chest of stories)—Ann Nellis

"Kubik." No one other one word describes him.—Philip Nenon & Tyler O'Halloran

Googler—Bill Robertson

Steadfast—Jamie Rauch

Intuitive—Josh Davis

Altruistic—unselfish concern for others—Beth Spann

Interested—John Henry

Incomparable—William Paulus

SUPERCALIFRAGILISTICEXPIALIDOCIOUS—Jon Alter

Empathetic—Jim Robertson

Inspirational—Sam Kendricks

Generous (of a person)—showing a readiness to give more of something, as money or time, than is strictly necessary or expected.—Kit Patterson

Loyal—Matt Scoggin

Friend—Ricky Berens

Genuine—Whitney Hedgepeth & Billy Humphries

Teammate—Elaine Calip

Heart—Carol Borgmann Robertson

Authentic—Mary Juarez

Effervescent—Wyatt Collins

Marvelous—Richard Sybesma

Relational—Wayne Madsen

Generous—Fran Robertson

JUST ONE???? You can't do that to a writer.  Humble—
Melanie Hauser

Spectacularlyamazing—Jill Sterkel

**Caring. Genius. Best. Selfless. Good. Friend.
Is that more than one word? I recruited
him 125 years ago. I get more words.**

---

 Chuck Warner

# CHAPTER 11

# Training

*If it was easy, everyone would do it.*

*Eddie with Doug Gjertsen and Adam Werth*

SUCCESS IN ANY FIELD RELIES ON A SOUND FOUNDATION of the fundamentals and principles of what and why things work the way they do in that profession. Coaching swimming is no different, and it is essential that one understands training methodologies and physiological responses and a myriad of other things that directly or indirectly relate to achieving success (speed) in the pool. In graduate school Eddie Reese thoroughly enjoyed his course work in physiology and the lab. The principles of the supercompensation curve were impressed upon him and helped him accurately evaluate the fatigue level in an athlete and whether the training load should be increased or decreased. Eddie was and is a student of the sport but also understands the old adage "all work and no play makes a dull boy."

**This sport is never easy. The better shape you get in, the more work you can do.**

"Protecting the mind" by injecting humor into each practice can be misleading in gauging the level of work his athletes consistently endure. However, it may well be his ability to bring joy to most experiences that enables his swimmers to sustain a regime that might feel like drudgery in another program.

At Auburn in the '70s, the transition into pool practice included a Frisbee game. With multiple discs flying across the pool, bouncing off the walls of the small room that housed the old pool, scores were tallied when a disc hit the deck. The air was filled with laughter before the work in the pool had ever begun. At Texas a game of "six-square" (an expanded version of four-square) is a regular pre-pool event that includes laughter, camaraderie, and plenty of trash talk.

**We had a lot of lawyers come out of it
because of all the arguments.**

A recently developed tradition is to start practice by having all the swimmers throw their snorkels at the backstroke flags at the far end of the pool. For every snorkel that hooks and stays, practice might start one minute later.

Once his swimmers are in the pool Eddie is still able to infuse humor into a long practice. Jeremy Harris '08 shares this:

*During a long course (50-meter) workout, Eddie was sitting on the block directly above my head, and before I pushed off to begin the main set he gleefully said, "Your ass is grass and I am the lawnmower."*

*I almost choked on water I was laughing so hard.*

John Martens remembers Eddie's "gift to the distance group."

*Before we got in the water, Eddie gathered all the distance guys in a circle to tell us the main set we're about to do. As he's speaking he gives the "claw" (elbow grab) to the guy to his left. This starts a chain reaction of each swimmer clawing the guy to his left and ending with Eddie being clawed.*

*We look at him and he cracks one of those smiles and starts*

 Chuck Warner

*laughing before giving us "the most fun" we've ever had—a really hard set.*

**There is a fine line between old school, new school, and dumb school. I'd rather stay on the old school side of that line.**

The coach's point is, in part, that jumping at new training ideas without careful thought is a mistake. Coaches can fall prey to a shiny new concept that might seem to work for the new fastest swimmer around but that might not help their swimmers.

**If you're not swimming bad at some time of the year, you're not trying to get better.**

In 2017 Coach Reese described the fall phase of his season with these monthly nicknames:

- *Socktember*—"because we wear mesh socks."
- *Rocktober*—"because I kill 'em in October."
- *Slowvember*—"because I killed them in October."

**Once you get an athlete to within three to five percent of their genetic gift, your margin of error is a lot less—you can't make any mistakes.**

One of the old school theories that Coach Reese has let go of is training his swimmers to the point that they become tired and slow for four or five months at a time. In recent years at Texas the season has included a rest that begins around Thanksgiving, in preparation for an early December invitational, at which time many Longhorns get their NCAA qualifying times out of the way.

Eddie's program is seldom "routine" from year to year. When he tried walking into practice once with the workout written out, it was so difficult and inflexible that "they had to bring ambulances to pick up the guys at the pool."

<blockquote>

**If you use the same stimuli, there's a real good chance a twenty-three-year-old will be slower, because there's no need to change. You have to apply different stimuli—different intensity, different length of time, all that stuff.**

</blockquote>

Bryan Jones '00 shares this example:

> *At the start of the season (fall) it's been a tradition to hold a "quadrathlon" each Saturday morning. (Every swimmer on the team races, in heats, from the blocks a timed 50 fly, then back, then breast, and finally freestyle.) I think in 1998 Eddie decided we needed to be better kickers. So he had us all wear sneakers on the kicking sets. On Saturday morning it was quite a sight to see each team member up on the blocks for the quadrathlon in shoes as well.*

Olympic team captain ('92, '96, 2000) Josh Davis swam for Eddie for nearly fourteen years and states, "I never did the same practice twice."

Eddie may repeat a set during a season, or a career, but never a total practice. In preparing for a workout, he will ponder sets, at times even talking with an athlete a day or two in advance about what to expect from a particularly challenging training day. Around his house one can find notes with a swimmer's initials and an idea for a set. His adjustments daily, weekly, and seasonally are a key part of his coaching genius.

Coaches are often described as authoritative or autocratic. Eddie Reese is a self-described "intuitive coach." The effect of intuition on planning and organization is analogous to the experience of hiking a spectacular outdoor trail. All five senses are active, smelling the trees and vegetation, seeing the waterfalls, hearing that water, grabbing and feeling a tree or rock for support, and even tasting a cool drink of water. But enjoyment of the total experience seldom involves conscious processing of thought.

Just like the hiker, Eddie's decisions are made from the inside out. He utilizes wisdom he has gained throughout his coaching career to generate training decisions, rather than following a fixed written plan. During a practice, it might take him three to five seconds to make his analysis, but for each of his thirty-plus swimmers he will walk the deck before, during, or after practice and adjust training for the individual: "Weights just Tuesday and Thursday this week," or, "No morning for you."

His approach succeeds because his swimmers trust his instincts rather than a graph or detailed plan that another coach might rely on.

**If you swim slow in practice you
become a good slow swimmer.**

As Coach Reese has gained experience his intuition has led him to a training program with repeats of shorter distances, so that swimmers swim closer to race speed more often.

Here is an interesting "ultra-short" yard set Coach Reese has used:

*Eight rounds every three minutes of (3 x 25s free on :15, 3 x 25s back/fly on :16, 3 x 25s breast on :18).*

A set that American record holding distance swimmer Clark Smith has done was:

*21 x 100s on 1:00, averaging 51.3 per 100.*

Many of Eddie's main sets will last forty-five minutes. For a distance swimmer, such a set could last well over an hour. An example of a set by Clark Smith is:

*800 yards easy on 8 min., 800 fast on 8 min., 700 easy on 7 min., 700 fast on 7 min., all the way down to 100. The total yardage is 7,200, lasting one hour and twelve minutes.*

**You have to have talent, work hard ... and it takes
time—and the time is different for everyone.**

Among the qualities we observed while coaching with Eddie at Texas, which has also been noted by others over the years, is Eddie's ability not only to determine what type of work or stimulus will help a swimmer but his patience to give that work or stress time to take effect.

Before George Block became a great friend of Eddie's, he had this experience:

*Very early on, my team was at a long course meet at the new UT pool. Probably a Senior Circuit meet. I think I was there with one boy and four girls. The boy was very talented and hardworking, but really green. I was doing my typical thing: working him hard and coaching him hard. By the fourth day, we were probably both getting a little frustrated with each other.*

*Eddie noticed.*

*In that little dead time after they clear the pool, but before the first heat, Eddie comes up behind me and tugs on my shirt sleeve. I turn around and it's Eddie, the "new" UT coach. He speaks slowly and softly, not quite a whisper and says, "There's no limit to how much that boy can improve, but there is a limit to how much he can improve in one season." Then he turns and walks away.*

*I think I was sort of pissed off at the time, something like, "Who the hell are you…?" It didn't take long to find out who the hell he was, but it probably took me a few more years to understand the wisdom of what he had just told me.*

> **All swim meets [races] measure where people are and who you've overtrained, so you don't make that same mistake at the end of the year.**

In addition to utilizing competitions to gauge his swimmers' adaptation to work, Eddie currently uses Tuesday and Friday practices to



Chuck Warner

assess his swimmers' ability to swim at "race tempo" for distances of 200 or less. In a set designed to provide enough rest to swim at race pace, he judges that tempo with his trained eye, rather than with any mechanical device.

One of Coach Reese's most unique abilities is to develop swimmers in all four strokes and the individual medley. Early in his career his swimmers were primarily successful—at the national and international levels—in distances of 200 or shorter. Over time, however, he's developed world class swimmers in the longer races, including Clark Smith's American records in the 500 and 1650 at the 2017 NCAA Championships.

Training progression might be summed up best in Coach Reese's words:

**At the end of our season I look at our guys and try to figure out what worked. If it did, I know it won't work the same way next year. So, I have to change it and make it harder. If it didn't, I have to discard it or figure out how to make it better.**

# CHAPTER 12

# Taper

*Taper is an art that no one understands.*

COACHING COMPETITIVE SWIMMING HAS MANY UNIQUE challenges, but none of them causes coaches to second guess themselves more than the decisions they make in the few weeks prior to their athletes' championship competition. This final preparation time is often referred to as the "taper." Even a coach with Eddie Reese's unparalleled success admits to an ongoing search for clarity in tapering each individual athlete.

 Chuck Warner

Most world class swimmers train many years for two seasons of twenty weeks or more each year, in a regimen that requires stressing them physically and psychologically four hours per day, six days per week. This is all done to prepare for a race that can last as little as twenty seconds or, at the most, fifteen minutes. A long, heavy workload is tapered down to a level that produces the energy needed for top performance in each specific event.

The dynamic art of tapering is often left up to the intuitive judgment of the coach. It is a process that, after completion, leaves even seasoned coaches scratching their heads, wondering if they've done right by their swimmers.

**Taper is determined by the length of your season, the difficulty of your practices, and the consistency of your swimmer in those practices.**

Coach Reese possesses an extraordinary sensitivity to the fatigue of an athlete. As the days count down toward the championship, he looks for a "relative sharpness" in each athlete that comes from dramatically decreasing the work in the final three to six weeks before the competition.

Eddie's ability to evaluate human performance spans beyond swimming into other sports.

Former Texas Athletic Director DeLoss Dodds (who wrote the foreword for this book) says, "Most coaches know *how* to work athletes hard, but Eddie knows *when* to work them hard. And he knows when to rest them to get the peak performance out of them."

Eddie shares this story:

*Years ago, when John Mackovic was football coach (at Texas), they were, I think, 3-2 after the first five games. He came out and said, "We're not finishing games well. We've got a week off, we're going to have to go back to work."*

*DeLoss Dodds told me, "We both know what's wrong with that."*

*He then told me, "You're the only one who can get away with talking to John."*

*So I went to him and his offensive coordinator. I said, "I've got one question: Are you starting your games slow and getting tired, or starting as fast as you should and getting tired?"*

*He said, "We're starting slow and finishing slow."*

*I said, "That means you're working too hard in between." So Coach Mackovic called off the hard work. His team won the Big 12 (conference championships).*

Ricky Berens '10, two-time Olympian and Olympic gold medalist, shares his experience with Coach Reese and Coach Dave Salo (assistant USA Olympic coach and head coach at the University of Southern California):

*Taper with Dave Salo is something very different. Eddie and Dave have two very different coaching styles, which means two different taper styles. Dave even has a different word for it, "the fine tuning stage."*

*… At Texas I felt like Eddie Reese gave us some of the longest tapers in the country. We would start probably five weeks out, sprinters a little longer, some days would be pace and other days would be a 3,000 on our own. I remember one Thursday at afternoon practice, because this swimmer swam very poorly at a dual meet, Eddie came into practice and told this kid to take the next three days off and "I will see you Monday afternoon." About two weeks later, the kid dropped a couple seconds in his 200 breast. Eddie's taper approach always amazed me.*

**I know for a fact that if you think about adding something within a three-week taper that will help them, you are wrong. Leave it alone and it will help them more. There is nothing [more] you can do.**

 Chuck Warner

During the season's final taper, most of his swimmers experience a withdrawal phase from the many months of consistent training. The transition is like a person withdrawing from a sugary diet, or even an alcoholic or drug addict going through withdrawal. When the routine stimulus stops, the consumer initially feels worse, not better. The same is true for most swimmers that trade their regular work habit for a period of increased rest and sharpening.

In a speech at the 1976 ASCA World Swim Coaches Clinic, Hall of Fame Coach Dick Jochums made this comment:

*I was sitting in the back of the room during Eddie Reese's talk and heard him say, "Give it time to work." When he said that I sat up and wrote a note, "rest and give the rest time to work." It takes time to taper. You have to give the rest time to work.*

### You can't rest too much, but you can rest too long.

How long is too long? Eddie has described training as a rocket being launched into space. He explains that initially it requires tremendous force to get that space ship blasting through the atmosphere. Even without any further force or training, it will continue to soar for a limited time before it begins to fall back toward earth. If a coach chooses to dramatically reduce the level of work or "rest a great deal," a highly trained athlete will still be able to perform well for a period—until their proverbial rocket, or training effectiveness, begins to fall.

Often swim coaches are unsure whether they have rested their athlete too long. Coach Reese often conducts time trials about four days after the championship. This allows him to observe his swimmers and consider whether the rest he chose for them was too long or perhaps not long enough.

### If they don't have muscle, they don't taper much.

As stated earlier, strength training is a critical aspect of the athlete's improvement. An individual's muscle mass can also predict how much rest is needed during the taper. The more the muscle mass, the longer the taper.

*Ian Crocker*

Ian Crocker '04 was a three-time Olympian, five-time Olympic medalist, and world record holder (2003–09) in the 100-meter butterfly. He also broke world records—in a short course meters pool—and qualified for an Olympic team in freestyle. Ian's season training and his tapers at Texas (2001–08 undergrad and post-grad) were challenging to formulate at first. After a disappointing freshman year at Texas (2001), he spent more time in the distance lane each fall and more time resting. This combination—distance training early and long tapers—isn't a common formula for success, but Eddie knows that every individual reacts differently to training and tapering.

In Eddie's view, an individual's sharpness is specific to each of the four strokes. He said the following in reference to tapering Ian Crocker:

**Racing freestyle takes more strokes, faster strokes,**



Chuck Warner

**so it makes sense to need more rest. Rest is not just muscular rest, it is neuromuscular rest. The nervous system takes longer to rest than the muscle side of it.**

During the collegiate season at Texas, most swimmers are out of the weight room three weeks prior to their championship. This time frame, however, can be very individualized.

**I do have a problem. It's hard to get them to stop (weights) when I want them to. And I will admit, when I have a doubt, they're out.**

Returning to the original statement that "Taper is an art that no one understands," Eddie says soberly:

**Sometimes you just have to make your best guess.**

———

# Why So Much Winning?

# Winning

*I can't tell you where any of the rings are that we've won, but I can tell you what everybody did and how much they improved that gave us a chance to win.*

*2016 NCAA Championship Team*

THE WINNING THAT HAS PERSISTED AT TEXAS IS UNPRECedented, not only in collegiate swimming, but for nearly any sport in the world. The incremental steps that Eddie and his teams have employed were in some ways prompted by the previous local champion, SMU.

The SMU program had a long tradition of success, both nationally and internationally. At the 1979 Southwestern Conference (SWC) Championships held at Texas, SMU carried out their longtime pre-meet ritual cheer of chanting out a series of numbers—"57! 58! 59!…"—all the way to "78!" The numbers signified the years that SMU had won the SWC meet, an unbroken streak from 1957 all the way to their most recent win in 1978.

When they finished at "78!" Eddie walked over to SMU Coach George McMillion ("Coach Mac") and in a low voice said, "George, this has gotta stop."

The next year at the 1980 SWC Championships, Texas stopped both the record and the cheer. The competition was fierce, but the Longhorns prevailed, ending SMU's twenty-two-year reign as SWC champions. Dana Abbott was an assistant coach at the time and shares this story:

*As is the custom at UT, the team was awarded Conference Championship rings. I went over to the athletic office to be measured for my ring. The secretary who was handling the sizing and the orders said, "You can have your initials, or whatever initials you would like engraved on the inside of the ring."*

*I quickly replied, "How about S-M-U?"*

*She cracked up and said, "You know, you're the second person to request that today."*

*I asked, "Who was the other?"*

*She just grinned and said, "Eddie."*

**Eighty percent like to win, twenty percent hate to lose, ninety-five percent of the Olympic team comes from the hate-to-lose group. So anybody that's ever been on an Olympic team, you assume they've got the killer instinct, which means they hate to lose. You always know they're gonna be great in a race.**

One of the transformative swimmers in those early years was Scott Spann. He was strong, fast, and his primary events were shorter distances, the 200-individual medley, 100 butterfly and 100 breaststroke. At the All-American Meet in January 1979,

 Chuck Warner

Eddie put Scott in one of the most difficult endurance races, the 200 butterfly, against soon-to-be world record holder in the 200-meter backstroke Rick Carey. Rick, trained by Coach John Collins (father of current UT assistant Wyatt), had tremendous endurance. But on the last fifty of the race, Scott found a way to beat Rick.

**That's why he's a champion.**

*'81 Men's Championship Team*

Eddie could recognize not only the physical ability but also the mental traits of champions like Scott Spann. After their first NCAA team title in 1981, the new American record holder in the 100-yard butterfly put into words what a lot of Eddie's swimmers have felt over the years. "I'd have gone to any school in the country if Ed was going," Spann said. "If the pool was only one lane that was twenty yards long, I would have gone. Fortunately for both of us, that didn't happen."

John Henry '81 was a part of the first NCAA Championship team at Texas.

*When we won in 1981 Eddie told me, "I didn't know we were going to win until we reached the turning point." Which begged my question, "When was that, Ed?" He said, "The 100 butterfly." Well since I was a 100 butterflyer, it made me feel great for thirty-plus years.*

*Fast forward to 2015, Hayden (my nephew) told me Eddie didn't think they were going to win "until we reached the turning point." Hayden asked, "When was that, Ed?" He said, "The 500 free." Ha! The first event. (I think that was the year Clark Smith tore up the 500.)*

**Somebody wished me luck the first day. I told them, "I don't want any luck. I just want to win the close ones." We did that, and that takes some special character.**

In the early '80s it was Cal, UCLA, and his brother Randy's teams at Florida that posed the stiffest competition for team titles. Decades later Eddie said that Texas' 1984 performance was one of their best ever, even though Florida beat the Longhorns by 10.5 points. The top Texas diver, also considered the best in the country, broke his nose in warmup and had another injury later on at the meet. Nonetheless, Eddie's assessment was that his guys swam best times in the preliminaries and faster in finals. That was all he could ask for.

By the mid to late '80s it was Stanford and Southern Cal that posed the biggest challenges. It took time, but in 1988 Texas notched their second NCAA Championship. And then it was three more in a row. Shaun Jordan '90 summed up his feelings this way: "Eddie Reese and Kris Kubik … Those guys are the reason we're swimming fast. See, we don't do things like shave in December or rest for dual meets, and we get our asses kicked. But Eddie says, 'Guys, remember that you're swimming for the payoff, and swimming at the end doesn't lie.'"

Another key member of the class of '90 was Doug Gjertsen. As they celebrated their third consecutive title, Doug explained his highlight: "When you can help fire up the younger guys to swim better and swim

 Chuck Warner

to their potential … lead by example: showing courage, showing guts, not backing down on the last twenty-five of a race."

**At my age, I don't remember the other five [titles]! I just take them one at a time.**

Stanford ran off with a few titles, but in 1996 it was Texas back on top again. As usual Eddie bore the pain of the "drought" and shouldered the responsibility for it when he said, "The last few years, we tapered by the book instead of going on a case-by-case basis with an intuitive feel."

When Texas superstar and top scorer Neil Walker heard of his coach's comments, he quipped, "The guy's finally learning."

*Neil Walker 2000 & 2004 Olympic Gold Medalist*

**Our philosophy has just been to keep it fun, to keep smiling, and keep laughing.**

But when Texas won again in 2000, the intensity of Longhorn swimmers' yearning for their day atop the awards podium like their brethren from years past was best expressed by Bryan Jones (who anchored three winning relays): "For three years we've been pretty much humiliated in the pool. We learned from that, and this year we did a great job of holding it together for three days. It's a great feeling to win a team title."

At the beginning of the 21$^{st}$ century, Texas won three in a row. Two-time Olympian Nate Dusing said, "No matter how bad you feel, no matter how much you hurt, you've got to do it for Texas."

Then David Marsh's Auburn teams reeled off five straight. During that time the Longhorns weren't just competing to win NCAA Championships, they were winning around the world. The decade of 2000–09 might be known as the period of "The Big Three": Aaron Peirsol, Brendan Hansen, and Ian Crocker. Their long careers on the world stage included swimming the first three legs of the gold medal 400 medley relay in Athens (2004), and all three athletes won gold in Beijing (2008) as well.

One of the great wins in Coach Reese's career was having his swimmers earn eight out of the twenty-one spots on the 2008 Men's Olympic team, a number unheard of in the last quarter century. Included in the group was Scott Spann's son (also named Scott), and Coach Kubik was named to assist on the USA staff. Perhaps it is Aaron Peirsol's mantra, "I prepare to win on my worst day," that best describes that amazing group of swimmers.

> **This [last night 2010] was one of our best final
> days, ever. The only thing special about it
> was the people that were doing the swims.**

In 2010 it was the Longhorns edging Cal, despite winning only one relay and one individual event. Ricky Berens '10 summed up his feelings: "We worked so hard every single day for the last four years, and we knew we were not going to come up short. To go out this way is amazing."

As the championships accumulated, Texas has developed a team tradition dictating the order in which swimmers jump into the pool to celebrate a national championship. First is the freshman class, followed by the sophomores, juniors, staff, and finally the senior class. In 2015 there was a delay as the entire team and staff waited for the senior class, who were huddled in a small hallway adjoining the pool deck. Kip Darmody, one of the senior team leaders, explained the holdup: "Only four of our eight-member senior class were at NCAAs. The four of us who were here needed to take a moment to reflect on the contribution of our fellow senior teammates."

*2018 Seniors, (L-R) Joseph Schooling, Brett Ringgold, Jonathan Roberts.*

The title run from 2015 to 2018 included individual American records by Jack Conger, Will Licon, Joe Schooling, and Clark Smith, in events from 100 to the 1650.

After the 2018 win senior Jonathan Roberts sounded a lot like Doug Gjertsen almost thirty years earlier: "Any stupidity that I can throw in, like taking my 400 IM out in 1:42 … it will get the fans going and get the team going … Leaving a mark on what a Texas Longhorn should look like has been one of the biggest honors of my life."

**I don't know that [there's pressure]. I don't feel it. I've never had to be an Olympic coach, never had a goal to win an NCAA, all I want to do is make him/her faster, you faster. Even if it kills you. I love that statement. We work real hard.**

Is it possible that a primary cause of so much winning is, in large part, the fact that they have paid so little attention to it?

Over the years Eddie has responded with patience to many of the challenges he has faced with swimmers, from missing classes to late nights that diminish their daily training efforts. Eddie has tried to observe a self-imposed forty-eight-hour cool-down period before he deals with the tougher discipline challenges, such as the one in the story that follows.

One season the Longhorns had a swimmer who, for unknown reasons, was reluctant to swim on relays. On the first day of the conference championships he asked to be left off a relay, even though he was the coach's certain choice to be on it. Rather than immediately confronting the conflict, Eddie obliged then waited until the final night of the competition, when he scheduled a meeting for the next morning with the young man, one of his parents, and Kris. Eddie and Kris did nearly all the talking.

The athlete apologized, but there was teaching to be done, and Eddie started in.

**As good as you are, you can't be that way. You are a beginner.**

Then he invoked some wisdom from Elinor. He explained that they had been helping a troubled young man and his family for twenty years. When the boy in the family was four years old, Elinor predicted

　　　　　Chuck Warner

he would eventually spend time in jail. The reason? His stubbornness. Eddie suggested a similarity in the way the swimmer behaved.

**I need you to be all in, and I need you to trust me.**

Kris underscored the team and tradition. "One of the happiest moments that I've heard from Eddie is when you told him in your goal meeting that you would replace the points lost by [a high scoring member of the previous year's team]."

**If you should win, you should win. I know that's
real simple and the equation to get there is
complex. Just be willing to race these guys.**

"If you're the best you can be, we're going to be proud of you," Kris continued. "You've got teammates that would give you a kidney if you needed it." He went on, "When *we* want you to do something for the team, it's not *we,* as in Eddie and me. It's all of your teammates and those alumni that keep hitting refresh on their computer waiting for our results [to update]."

**There is something inside you that draws you
to swimming. You have found the sport you
are best at. I want you to enjoy it more.**

Coach Kubik: "Twenty to thirty years from now you're going to remember singing 'The Eyes of Texas' in there [the locker room], not how fast you went."

**I really appreciate you apologizing.**

"We're not perfect, and everything doesn't go perfectly," Kris emphasized. "Something will go wrong at NCAAs. Maybe it's a relay disqualification, but we're not going home [if that happens]."

**We generally know the right choice,
and it's the hardest one.**

Kris concluded, "We've had meetings like these many times on different subjects. I believe in you and believe you will live what you've said."

**You have so much to give … just give us your best …
Whatever has happened in the past is forgotten.**

Eddie urged selflessness in the young man by explaining that people who give their time to work with the homeless are in fact the ones receiving the gift. When you invest in others or help others, it makes you better. He stood up and hugged the swimmer.

**To do something that has never been done you
have to do something that's never been done.**

The swimmer proceeded to train like no one ever has. Within two years he won an Olympic Gold Medal—on a relay.

*Michael Hixon, Coach Scoggins, Michael Bower*

**Don't do it like that again.**

Or so suggests Eddie Reese to a UT diver that flops a dive in practice.

                    Chuck Warner

The UT NCAA team titles have always been earned in both swimming *and* diving. "Eddie seems to think he's a great diving coach, and who are we to tell him any different?" diving coach Matt Scoggin '85 says with a smile. "Eddie is one of the greatest coaches in any sport there has ever been. He knows what's important to each person and wants to make sure that part of their life is in order. Then we have fun outworking everyone else."

Most Fridays the swimmers and divers meet in the locker room for a "clap session." They go around the room sharing their high achievements of the week, be they academic, diving related, or swimming related. The shared stories from each individual are affirmed with two claps by their swimming and diving teammates.

The formula for the success of the Texas swimming program has been for talented, competitive swimmers to invest in hard work and in each other and to trust the decisions of their coaches. Together they engage in a process of growth as people and as swimmers. Coach Reese's expectations of small, incremental improvements each day, both as a person and as an athlete, have translated into huge advances over time.

Jim Pullin '03 shares this story:

*When I was ten years old I had this dream that I wanted to be a part of an NCAA Championship swim team. I made five official college visits and made at least another five unofficially. There was one reason and one reason only that I ventured from Ohio down to Austin to swim at The University of Texas: Eddie Reese. He showed great interest in me, in my family, and sold me on how he could help me reach my potential.*

*My freshman year (2000) we won the NCAA team title, but I didn't qualify to go to the meet. My sophomore year I won the Big 12 Championships in the 1650 in a time that I was pleased with (15:14.75). I climbed out of the pool, very excited, and Eddie and Kris were standing right there. They congratulated me, and then Eddie said, "You can go faster."*

Eddie and Kris were concerned that Jim's time was about two seconds slow of what would qualify for NCAAs. They worked out signals with Jim for the pace he would need to swim a little faster. After Jim swam 800 yards his chances looked slim. He battled through 1000 yards, giving everything he had, but he was exhausted and way off the pace needed to qualify. Finally Eddie gave the signal to Jim to stop because he wasn't going to improve his time. Jim couldn't bring himself to stop in front of the crowd.

Eddie Reese, clad in his best coaching attire for the final night of the championships, walked to the starting block of Jim's lane and stood on top. The team and the staff wondered what in the world he was doing. Eddie Reese knows that experiencing pain in training and racing is a part of the sport. He expects his athletes to hurt. But he didn't want Jim Pullin to continue with this kind of pain.

As Jim turned at 1125 yards, Eddie extended his arms in a streamline over his head. When Jim was about ten yards from the starting block, Eddie jumped into the pool fully clothed in front of Jim to stop him. Eddie said, "You don't need to go on," and then he hugged Jim Pullin.

After the competition concluded, an emotional Texas team met in a circle in the locker room. Taking a lesson of compassion and complete support for one another from their teacher, they each took a turn expressing how much they loved each other. When the circle was complete, the coaches got up and exited the locker room. Kris said to Eddie, "It really doesn't matter what place we get at NCAAs in three weeks, because we all just won something

          Chuck Warner

better than any kind of trophy tonight."

As it worked out, Jim did qualify for the NCAAs. A few weeks later Texas won title number eight by a huge margin.

For the last fifty-two years Eddie Reese has wrapped his arms not only around his swimmers but around fellow coaches and the entire sport. He has hugged us all.

# Take care of yourself, take care of each other, and the rest will take care of itself.

# Chapter 14

# A Living Legacy

*We have a great culture.*

Since Texas won their first title in 1981, seven other universities have also won one or more men's swimming championship, but capturing fourteen of them, as well as eleven runner-up, and seven third-place finishes, is the result of an ongoing legacy. Winning the 2001 title necessitated out-swimming and out-diving a tremendous Stanford team. Eddie's guys won eleven events and set six American records. The performances then, just like the performances since, have been the result of a self-perpetuating process of one Longhorn swimmer leading the next toward finding their personal potential and contributing to their team's continuing success.

In short, culture eats strategy for breakfast.

The instigator of that culture is Eddie Reese. In addition to Eddie, Kris, and the coaching staffs, the senior classes and team captains often provide magnificent leadership, each class contributing a link from one championship to the next.

Marty Hubbell '96 offers his perspective: "My freshman year I had two captains, Daniel Watters and Doug Dickinson, who taught me

　Chuck Warner

from the very beginning what was expected of you as a Texas swimmer."

In the pool, leaders of each stroke pass a baton full of training and racing wisdom every few years. For example, in freestyle Kris Kirchner was an NCAA champion ('81) and Olympian ('80) who modeled world class qualities to John Smith, who modeled them for Doug Gjertsen and Shaun Jordan. Over the years Josh Davis, Neil Walker, Nate Dusing, Jamie Rauch, Garrett Weber-Gale, Ricky Berens, Dave Walters, Clark Smith, and Townley Haas are a few names among many who have received from their predecessors and given to their successors their personal acumen for swimming as fast as possible in the freestyle events.

*Townley Haas and Clark Smith,*
*American Record Holders and Olympic Gold Medalists*

Forty years of Texas history links William Paulus to Crocker to Schooling and Conger in the butterfly, and Spann to Stackle to Hansen to Licon in breaststroke. Backstroke history connects NCAA champion Clay Britt in the early eighties to Walker to Thibault to Peirsol to John Shebat and to Austin Katz in 2018.

*Brendan Hansen and Will Licon: American Records in Breaststroke*

Each athlete feels the casual humanity of the routine of training, racing, traveling with, and befriending their Longhorn teammates, some of whom are the best swimmers in the world. They witness first-hand the consistent commitment to hard work necessary to achieve one's potential and, when possible, win Olympic gold medals. Over time they have collectively created a legacy that lives today.

Bryan Jones '00 says, "Eddie directs the team, but it's often the upperclassmen that teach. It might be starts, it might be turns, it might be how to handle college life, but there was a tradition of passing on lessons to teammates before I came to Texas. It continues today."

Following the 2001 victory celebration, Jamie Rauch prodded Coach Kubik for a t-shirt to honor their championship. Instead, Jamie and his teammates received something more than they could have imagined. Kris solicited letters from many of their forerunners on UT swim teams and bound them into a gift book for that 2001 squad. The names of some of the authors of those letters might be familiar to you, but many won't be. Their relative obscurity represents the value of a superbly conducted collegiate athletic expe-



Chuck Warner

rience. Most never became Olympians and some never qualified to perform at the NCAA Championships. But their passion and determination in passing the torch to succeeding classes can't be overlooked or underestimated.

Who better to touch upon the legacy they built in those first twenty-three years than the athletes themselves?

These excerpts of their written thoughts and perspectives after decades away from their time at UT bear testimony to the life skills they gained as dedicated athletes on a Texas team.

**Bill Robertson '82:** "How appropriate that on the twentieth anniversary of UT's first NCAA Swimming and Diving victory you too have reached the top. It's hard to believe that half of you were not even born when we won that first one."

**Kelly Rives '82:** "Eddie and Kris took a chance on me back in 1978 and I took a leap of faith. Ed said we were a team and were going places … Only years from now will you truly realize what you did."

**John Kenny '82:** "I know that as a member of the '81 National Championship team a day hardly goes by that I don't reflect upon my swimming days with pride."

**Mike Wilson '84:** "Today, you are heroes. To the people you go to school with. To the people who love you. To Eddie and Kris. To all the guys that went before you who thrashed out workouts in that damned pool. Enjoy this. Accept our awe, congratulations, admiration, and respect. And know, this is the time of your lives."

**Coach Matt Scoggin '85:** "I have been a part of very talented teams that did not win the title. You all worked way beyond the norm, and I am proud to be a part of a team that worked their tails off for the title, not sitting back and trying to collect on talent alone."

**'Becca Scoggin (coach's wife):** "For two sports that really have nothing to do with each other except get wet in a well of water, you all obviously recognize the importance of the team aspect. It may be hard to appreciate now, but every collegiate swimming and diving team would love to have swimmers that support divers and vice versa."

**Bill Stapleton '87:** "I remember in high school, in a farming town in southern Illinois, how cool I thought I was [and I was] wearing my UT Swimming t-shirt from my recruiting trip. That shirt meant something important … It meant I was a part of something bigger than myself, with expectations of greatness … You have no idea what their [Eddie's and Kris's] guidance will mean in your lives going forward, as students, as professionals, and most importantly as fathers."

**Spencer Martin '88:** "Whether any particular individual had the meet of his life, or whether he was not on top form, all of that will surprisingly soon be forgotten or nearly so. It's mainly the team achievement that lives on, and that's what makes college swimming so special relative to anything else you will do."

**Patrick Brundage '89:** "You'll all come to realize and you all contribute to the almost 'mystical' power of that word 'Texas' in the swimming world … I'm still searching for a company that has leadership like Eddie and Kris … and I haven't found it yet."

**Jeff Olsen '90:** "When you consider how far across the globe Longhorn swimmers have had the opportunity to travel—representing the USA and The University—you realize it is an understatement to say 'The Eyes of Texas Are Upon You.' Indeed, the eyes of the world are often upon the Longhorn swimming family."

**Adam Werth '91:** "I think this is the fifth-best team in the history of Texas Swimming & Diving … I was joking, but I think everybody who has ever competed for UT cherishes those years and feels that their time spent there has instilled an incredible amount of pride … We've all built a tradition. A tradition that I think rivals any in sports today."

**Dave McClellan '90:** "My kudos go out … not just to the event champions and record breakers, but also to every swimmer on the team who poured his heart and soul into every swim, weight, and dryland workout throughout the year."

**Jeff Thibault '92:** "Thank you for making me proud to be a UT alum and taking this program to an unprecedented level."

**Daniel Watters '92:** "I was so proud to be wearing the Orange and White when the team trophies were handed out and even Stanford stood and applauded our team."

**Jonathan Jennings '94:** "Men, when you want to know how to lead, you have the best models on your pool deck every day. I hope you understand what a privilege and honor it is to have such fine gentleman [Eddie and Kris] literally give all of who and what they are to you, on a daily basis."

**Marty Hubbell '96:** "To know you've accomplished a team goal [NCAA title] is one thing. To know that you have done it the right way, to the satisfaction of those who came before you, is quite another."

Another six NCAA Team Championships have followed since, but the formula for classes passing down expectations, accountability, and success has remained the same.

> **We know swimming isn't life or death, and
> we're not going to treat it that way.**

In 2011 William Paulus '83 was inducted into the Longhorn Hall of Honor for a career that included a world record in the 100-meter butterfly. On that occasion Dr. Paulus (now an orthodontist) said, "It's not just what I did myself, but everyone I was around did that same thing. Whether they won something or set a world record, they still reached their potential in the sport and outside of it, which is kind of unusual in a lot of places."

> **When you have a year like this, with people
> like this, you think you can do this forever.**

---

# Chapter 15

# Around the Corner

*I think I'm probably funnier now than I've ever been. That's purely a personal opinion.*

*Ricky Berens and Coach Reese*

IN 2011 THERE WAS A TIME WHEN THE JOKES STOPPED. Walking up the ramp toward a basketball game at The University of Texas, Eddie felt faint. Elinor got him to the hospital, where he underwent triple bypass surgery.

**I'm fixed. It's like that country song: I'm not afraid of dying, but I don't want to do it today.**

Eddie Reese couldn't know what would happen walking up that

ramp, nor can any of us know what's around the corner. That experience was an emphatic reminder for him to attend to good nutrition and fitness. When Elinor and Eddie turned seventy years young they decided to have the mindset of living like they were in their fifties.

**If I didn't have mirrors in my house, I wouldn't know that I was old—until I go upstairs.**

Coach Reese's exercise routine is admirable, even for a much younger man. On Monday, Wednesday, and Friday he awakens at 4:45 a.m. and performs 200 exercises (a combination of pushups, sit-ups, etc.) and walks his dogs before making the twenty-minute drive to the Jamail Texas Swimming Center for 6 a.m. practice. Back at home each night he rides his exercise bike for an hour and walks his dogs again. And he still climbs the steep steps up the football stadium to reach the weight room and lifts weights three times a week with his swimmers, which maintains the strength he needs to lift fifty-pound bags of corn to fill his deer feeder.

**I like being on the cutting edge of training, nutrition, weight lifting, and I like trying to find new and better ways to do things.**

Learning how to be a more effective coach keeps Eddie stimulated.

**I've either been cursed or blessed with a gene that demands you find a way to get better.**

Joseph Campbell, the mythology expert who helped inspire the Star Wars movies, once paraphrased 1 Corinthians 8:2 when he said, "He who thinks they know, doesn't know. He who knows they don't know, *knows*." That describes Eddie Reese. This coach is constantly looking for any idea, from anybody and anywhere, that will help his swimmers improve. Each day he attempts to help his swimmers reach their potential, he also strives for his own excellence as a coach.

Eddie has been gracious enough to agree to a couple of in-depth public interviews with me at the ASCA World Clinic over the last ten years. Most recently (2017) he confided, "I'm afraid if I retire, I'll look back in a few years and realize how many silly mistakes I made that, had I done it differently, my swimmers could have been faster."

When he headed back to Austin, Eddie sent me a text from the airport: "Thanks … my current challenge is to understand why my good guys are improving nicely but my other guys are not as much as I'd like. Any ideas?"

**You can't make it happen. You can allow it to happen.**

All athletes' common goal is to have "peak performances," in which they perform very close to or at their potential. These experiences are most meaningful when the preparation investment has been enormous and the event is special to the athlete. A great coach enables athletes to realize these moments that tell them something about their harmony in being alive. This experience of touching one's personal greatness, even if it happens rarely, is vividly instilled in an athlete's memory forever.

*Joseph Schooling*

     Chuck Warner

Eddie Reese's coaching excellence has directly helped thousands of swimmers touch a moment of greatness in their lives and tens of thousands indirectly by "coaching coaches" around the world.

**I'm going to go before anyone wants me to go, but the guys are still laughing at my jokes. I am getting better. I want all my swimmers going fast.**

Wisdom has been defined as knowledge plus experience. As Coach Reese continues to learn and gain experience from additional seasons with additional athletes, he has improved his effectiveness with his swimmers. He has also served as a resource to all of us, not only for coaching but, more importantly, for teaching and living.

When the subject comes up of retiring to do other things, Eddie responds that he has always balanced coaching with other activities. Elinor, quick with a quip herself, asks, "Why stop working when you never have?"

**If I can't go fishing, I like to talk about it.**

Venturing off into nature has always been important to Eddie. His hobbies have long included hunting and fishing, and at times they've been a priority. By the Olympic year of 1984, his team had won their first NCAA team title and his swimmers were beginning to perform at a world class level in the summer long course season. He was asked to be a part of the USA Olympic staff for the Los Angeles Games, but he had no interest. He went fishing instead.

At the opening of the American Swimming Coaches Association's World Clinic in 2017, he did address a few age issues he now faces:

**I've been to the NCAAs so many times I can spell it.**

**When I go to the ATM and it says, "put your card in and pull it out quickly," I'm beginning to worry that I won't be fast enough to make the transaction.**

**I paid to watch the [hugely promoted] McGregor-Mayweather fight on TV Saturday night and fell asleep before it started.**

In 1996 the Longhorn Foundation decided to make an exception to their policy of waiting until a coach has retired before inducting them into the Hall of Honor. DeLoss Dodds explained, "Eddie Reese's program stands for everything that is right with collegiate athletics and The University of Texas Athletic Department. The priority of developing people has created a by-product of winning championships ... Eddie told me that Kris Kubik is just as important to their success as he is." In 2011 Kris Kubik was also inducted while still coaching.

When Kris decided to retire after the 2016 Olympic Trials, he and Eddie jointly told twenty-six-year old volunteer assistant coach Wyatt Collins that they would like him to succeed Kris. Wyatt explained, "My entire life changed in five minutes. I am so grateful."

 Chuck Warner

*Wyatt Collins continues the Kubik tradition of
drying a block for a UT relay.*

Dana and I thought if we were going to soak up some of UT swimming while Eddie was still coaching, we ought to visit our old boss and did so in November of 2016.

I got to practice ahead of Dana. Immediately I introduced myself to Wyatt and said, "I'm here to check up on you and make sure you're getting the job done!" After a laugh, I asked about recruiting and how he was handling the big question most recruits would have. "How long will Eddie keep coaching?" Wyatt explained that it was tough to answer but pointed out Eddie's love of coaching and attention to good health.

I posed, "How about asking them, 'even if it would be for one year, wouldn't you want to swim for not only one of the greatest *swimming coaches* who has ever lived, but also one of the greatest coaches in *any sport* that has ever walked the planet?'

Wyatt smiled and said, "I like that a lot better."

Coach Reese has been compared to John Wooden, the prodigious basketball coach from UCLA. Both men have not only won the most national team titles in their respective sports but also had an enormous positive effect on the people they coached. Coach Wooden often repeated a poem he learned in school that describes both men:

*"No written word,*
*No spoken plea,*
*Can teach our youth what they should be,*
*Nor all the books on all the shelves,*
*It's what the teachers are themselves."*

*Eddie and the University of Georgia's coach Jack Bauerle*

In Joseph Schooling's senior speech at the 2018 Texas team banquet, he said, "Eddie is the purest man I know."

Jack Bauerle, head coach at Georgia (seven NCAA team titles and 2008 Olympic head coach) and close friend of Eddie's, not only believes Eddie is one of the best coaches ever, in any sport, but takes it a step further, "The gigantic and most important quotient of it all is that he is a genuinely great person in every regard. My life has been richer with him."

Preparing young people for life after swimming or what is "around the corner" in their lives has been the most important subject in Eddie Reese's teaching curriculum. His daughter Heather says that when she and her husband notice they are getting angry or frustrated, they often stop, look at each other, and say, "What would we do if we were Eddie Reese?" His swimmers and former assistant coaches express similar sentiments.

Kris Kubik looks back: "I walked on to the pool deck every day and worked with a true genius. It would be like being an associate scientist with Albert Einstein or having John Wooden standing next to you."

Jim Pullin is now a business owner and happily married man in Seattle, WA. He says, "Most coaches can tell you what to do, but Eddie also *shows* you what to do. About once a year he actually got in the pool and showed us things. I was invited with my other teammates who were far from home to his house each year for Thanksgiving. In that setting, he showed me how to treat your family, and I learned how to treat my wife."

Coach Reese has left in his streaming wake a lifelong effect on coaches and swimmers. His coaching career will come to an end at some point, but what he has taught will carry on. Hundreds of former swimmers and past assistant coaches are now contributing to the lives of thousands of youngsters.

Neil Caskey explains his own career choice to coach swimming: "There's a saying that goes something along the lines of 'You can measure the impact of a coach by how many of his or her athletes go on to coach.' It was during my time at Texas, swimming for Eddie and Kris, that I decided I wanted to become a coach. If I can make a fraction of the impact on the athletes that I coach that they made on me, I'll call it a success."

Brendan Hansen, now Coach Hansen, says simply what many former swimmers who are now coaches feel: "The greatest compliment I could ever receive is for someone to say, 'you coach like Eddie Reese or Kris Kubik.'"

Eddie continues to open his eyes early in the morning with a smile on his face, ready to go help people swim faster. His blessing, and ours, is that his energy for coaching swimming and teaching life continues to bring him joy.

TEXAS
speedo

When you die, the only thing
you take with you is that which
you've given others. That's the
ballgame right there. What
if we're all able to do that?

In the fall of 1978 we pulled our cars into Austin, Texas, rented a room, threw a mattress on the floor, spent late nights busing or waiting tables, and returned soda bottles to stores for food or gas money so that we could learn from Coach Reese. A year or two of poverty to learn from Eddie was the greatest investment we could make in our lives. One might call it our personal fork in the road.

Creating this book may put us in the same financial place that we started in forty years ago, but the lessons from Eddie Reese are important for all to learn, be they coaches or simply individuals on a path of growth. Eddie likes to say that people who give are really the receivers. We've received tremendously by writing this book.

*Coaching the 1978 Orange and White Meet (L-R) Warner and Abbott. Our squad finished second. The picture is damaged from flooding to Dana's house from Hurricane Harvey in 2017. When Eddie heard of the damage, he messaged Dana saying, "Let me know what you need and I will bring it to you."*

## Class of 2022 (times as of 7/1/18)

Fungairino, Aitor Yards: 500 Free 4:24.03, 200 Free 1:35.12, 100 Free 44.21
LCM: 400 Free 4:02.11, 200 Free 1:50.60, 100 Free 51.99

Kibler, Drew Yards: 500 Free 4:14.72, 50 Free 19.38, 200 Free 1:32.65, 100 Free 42.9
LCM: 400 Free 3:54.49, 50 Free 22.80, 200 Free 1:49.04, 100 Free 50.00

Koustik, Andrew Yards: 500 Free 4:19.14, 400 IM 3:58.30, 100 Breast 54.83, 200 Fly 1:43.69
LCM: 400 Free 4:04.98, 400 IM 4:32.42, 100 Fly 54.54, 200 Fly 1:58.15

Krueger, Daniel Yards: 50 Free 19.48, 200 Free 1:35.58, 100 Breast 55.66, 100 Free 42.50
LCM: 50 Free 22.89, 200 Free 1:53.62, 100 Free 49.35

Park, Jason Yards: 100 Fly 46.99, 100 Back 47.09, 200 Back 1:43.17
LCM: 100 Fly 56.16, 100 Back 56.02, 200 Back 2:02.96

Scheinfeld, Charlie Yards: 200 IM 1:49.42, 100 Breast 53.63, 200 Breast 1:55.94
LCM: 200 IM 2:11.21, 100 Breast 1:03.42, 200 Breast 2:18.52

Willenbring, Matt Yards: 500 Free 4:21.71, 200 IM 1:44.14, 200 Free 1:35.84, 100 Free 43.22
LCM: 400 Free 3:58.84, 200 IM 2:02.72, 200 Free 1:51.91, 100 Free 49.17

Zettle, Alexander Yards: 500 Free 4:18.65, 200 Free 1:36.22, 1650 Free 15:20.36
LCM: 400 Free 3:51.44, 200 Free 1:49.13, 1500 Free 16:14.82

| YEAR | CHAMPION | COACH | SCORE | RUNNER-UP | POINTS | LOCATION |
|---|---|---|---|---|---|---|
| 2018 | Texas | Eddie Reese | 449 | California | 437.5 | Minneapolis |
| 2017 | Texas | Eddie Reese | 542 | California | 349 | Indianapolis |
| 2016 | Texas | Eddie Reese | 541.5 | California | 351 | Atlanta |
| 2015 | Texas | Eddie Reese | 528 | California | 399 | Iowa City |
| 2014 | California | David Durden | 468.5 | Texas | 417.5 | Austin |
| 2013 | Michigan | Mike Bottom | 480 | California | 406.5 | Indianapolis |
| 2012 | California | David Durden | 535.5 | Texas | 491 | Seattle |
| 2011 | California | David Durden | 493 | Texas | 470.5 | Minneapolis |
| 2010 | Texas | Eddie Reese | 500 | California | 469.5 | Columbus |
| 2009 | Auburn | Richard Quick | 526 | Texas | 487 | College Station |
| 2008 | Arizona | Frank Busch | 500.5 | Texas | 406 | Seattle |
| 2007 | Auburn | David Marsh | 566 | Stanford | 397 | Minneapolis |
| 2006 | Auburn | David Marsh | 480.5 | Arizona | 440.5 | Atlanta |
| 2005 | Auburn | David Marsh | 491 | Stanford | 414 | Minnesota |
| 2004 | Auburn | David Marsh | 634 | Stanford | 377.5 | Long Island |
| 2003 | Auburn | David Marsh | 609.5 | Texas | 413 | Austin |
| 2002 | Texas | Eddie Reese | 512 | Stanford | 501 | Athens |
| 2001 | Texas | Eddie Reese | 597.5 | Stanford | 457.5 | College Station |
| 2000 | Texas | Eddie Reese | 538 | Auburn | 385 | Minneapolis |
| 1999 | Auburn | David Marsh | 467.5 | Stanford | 414.5 | Indianapolis |
| 1998 | Stanford | Skip Kenney | 599 | Auburn | 394.5 | Auburn |
| 1997 | Auburn | David Marsh | 496.5 | Stanford | 340 | Minnesota |
| 1996 | Texas | Eddie Reese | 479 | Auburn | 443.5 | Texas |
| 1995 | Michigan | Jon Urbanchek | 561 | Stanford | 475 | Indianapolis |
| 1994 | Stanford | Skip Kenney | 566.5 | Texas | 445 | Minnesota |
| 1993 | Stanford | Skip Kenney | 520.5 | Michigan | 396 | Indianapolis |
| 1992 | Stanford | Skip Kenney | 632 | Texas | 356 | Indianapolis |
| 1991 | Texas | Eddie Reese | 476 | Stanford | 420 | Texas |
| 1990 | Texas | Eddie Reese | 506 | Southern California | 423 | Indianapolis |
| 1989 | Texas | Eddie Reese | 475 | Stanford | 396 | Indianapolis |
| 1988 | Texas | Eddie Reese | 424 | Southern California | 369.5 | Indianapolis |
| 1987 | Stanford | Skip Kenney | 374 | Southern California | 296 | Texas |



Chuck Warner

| YEAR | CHAMPION | COACH | SCORE | RUNNER-UP | POINTS | LOCATION |
| --- | --- | --- | --- | --- | --- | --- |
| 1986 | Stanford | Skip Kenney | 404 | California | 335 | Indianapolis |
| 1985 | Stanford | Skip Kenney | 403.5 | Florida | 302 | Texas |
| 1984 | Florida | Randy Reese | 287.5 | Texas | 277 | Cleveland State |
| 1983 | Florida | Randy Reese | 238 | SMU | 227 | Indianapolis |
| 1982 | UCLA | Ron Ballatore | 219 | Texas | 210 | Wisconsin |
| 1981 | Texas | Eddie Reese | 259 | UCLA | 189 | Texas |
| 1980 | California | Nort Thornton | 234 | Texas | 220 | Harvard |
| 1979 | California | Nort Thornton | 287 | Southern California | 227 | Cleveland State |
| 1978 | Tennessee | Ray Bussard | 307 | Auburn | 185 | Long Beach State |

# TRAINING SETS

*Training Samples from Eddie Reese's Program at Texas*

**<u>Saturday 9/10/16</u>**

Quadrathlon Example (3rd week of practice)

    Dive: 4 x 50 @ 10:00… IM Order, the guys timed for each other

***Joe Schooling:***

    20.8, 22.5, 25+, 20.9

***John Shebat:***

    22.3, 22.2, 27.3, 20.5

***Jack Conger:***

    21.5, 22.7, 28.8, 20.1

**<u>Early Season</u>**

***Brendan Hansen Breaststroke Sets 2004-08***

Aerobic set, short course yards:

    P – 400 Breast on 7 min

    S – 5 x 100s Fr on 1:15

    S – 6 x (150 Fr + 150 Breast)

    Pull 2 x 300 Breast on 5:15, then P 4 x 200s Fr on 2:30

    Pull 3 x 200 Breast on 3:30, then K 3 x 300s Br on 5:30

    Pull 4 x 100 Breast on 1:45, then S 4 x 400s Br on 6:00

Anaerobic set, short course yards:

    1 x 100 breast (HARD) on 1:10, 1 x 50 breast ez on 1:05

    2 x 100 breast (HARD) on 1:10, 2 x 50 breast ez on 1:05

    3 x 100 breast (HARD) on 1:10, 3 x 50 breast ez on 1:05

    4 x 100 breast (HARD) on 1:10, 4 x 50 breast ez on 1:05

Second set/different day:

    4 x (100 breast fast on 1:30, 50 breast fast on 1:00, 50 free ez on 1:30)

<u>**Tuesday 12/13/16**</u>

***Townley Haas – birthday get out swim***
Low volume day with main set of kicking with Sox
    150 Free, "Must swim faster than 1:10"
    9.37, 20.85, 43.71 (22.86), 1:07.25 (23.54)


<u>**Tuesday 1/31/17**</u>
2 x Broken 500s as 5 x 100s on 1:20 (in heats)

***Townley Haas***
    1)52.0, 52.0, 52.0, 52.1, 51.4
    2)50.1, 49.4, 49.5, 49.8, 49.4

Followed by,
    4 x 50s on 1 – 25.1, 25.5, 26.0, 25.7
    4 x 50s on 1 – 22.9, 22.9, 22.9, 22.8

***Jeff Newkirk***
    1) 52.0, 52.6, 52.0, 52.1, 51.7
    2) 50.7, 49.9, 49.5, 49.8, 49.4

Followed by,
    25.1, 25.5, 25.6, 25.5
    22.7, 22.7, 22.6, 22.6


<u>**Friday, 3/17/17 (In tech suits) – Taper**</u>

***Tate Jackson***
Dive 50 to foot touch on 40, 19.8
    25 to foot touch on 25, 10.3
    25 to hand touch 10.2
    Dive 50 fly, 21.3

***John Shebat***
Start 50 bk to flip on :45, 21.7
    Push 25 to hand on :30, 10.7
    Push 25 to finish, 10.4

***Brett Ringgold***
4 x 50s free on :50, push
    22.7, 22.5, 22.2, 21.8
3 x 50s free on :45, Dive 1, push 2 & 3
    20.9, 22.4, 22.2
50 fly Dive
    21.5

## Friday, 2017

***Clark Smith***
    5 x 100s on 1:00, 100 ez on 3
    4 x 100s on 58, 100 ez on 3:08
    3 x 100s on 56, 100 ez on 3:12
    3 x 100s on 55, 100 ez on 3:15
    3 x 100s on 54, 100 ez on 3:18
    3 x 100s on 53, 150 ez on 5
    3 x 100s on 52 (49, 51, 50), 100 ez
    3 x 100s on 51, 100 ez

## Friday, 2017

***Joe Schooling***
2 x 6 x 50s fly (w/fast suit, push-off)
Rnd 1/Rnd 2
    1 on 1:00, 21.6/21.7
    2 on 1:15, 22.8, 22.6/22.5, 22.2
    3 on 1:30, 22.5, 22.2, 22.0/22.3, 22.0, 21.9

## Saturday 3/6/17

***John Roberts***
Broken 400 IM
    2 x 50s on 50, 2 x 50s on 50, 2 x 50s on 55, 2 x 50s on 45
    fly, 24.0, 24.6/ bk, 24.9, 24.6/ br, 29.3, 29.4/ fr, 23.1, 23.2

*Ricky Berens*
From a push off wall:
> 20 x 50 – odds kick on :35, evens swim on :30.
> He was about :31 on the kicks and :25 on the swims.

From a Dive wearing a jammer:
> 5 x 200 butterfly on 10:00. 1) 1:52 2) 1:46 on next four. Asked if he could do one more and with whole team cheering him on, he went 1:44.2.

> 300 free, 150 free, 100 free, 50 free.  The whole team did the set so there were about five heats. Interval was whenever all five heats finished the 300s they then started five heats of 150s, etc.
> He went free and went 2:26, 1:06, :44, and :20. After set he challenged two guys to a 100 free.  He went 42.6

## Distance Swimmer Michael Klueh Season Progression (2007-08)
> Michael finished the season with best yard times of 200, 1:33.62, 500, 4:10.00, 1650,14:36.07.

## December
> 8 x 50 on :45  (:27), 800 on 8:30 (7:20), 6 x 50 on :50 (:26), 600 on 6:30 (5:20)
> 4 x 50 on :55 (:25), 400 on 4:30 (3:31), 2 x 50 on 1:00, 1 x 200 on 2:30 (1:46)

> 4 x 100 on :55 (:51. :52. :53, :53), 5 x 50 on :45 (:30), 4 x 200 on 1:50 (1:46, 1:47, 1:46, 1:46), 5 x 50 on :45 (:30), 3 x 300 on 3:00, 5 x 50 on :45, 2 x 400 on 4:00, 5 x 50 on :45, 1 x 500 on 5:00

> 2 x (50 on :30 (:25), 100 on 1:00 (:54), 150 on 1:30 (1:21), 200 on 2:00 (1:49), 250 on 3:00 (2:18), 300 on 3:00 (2:41))

> 11 x 175 on 1:45  (150 pace, 25 ez)  add 150s for a 1650 time (14:32)

3000 on 30:00 (28:58), 6 x 50 on :45 (:27), 2000 on 20:00 (18:53), 6 x 50 on :45 (:27), 1000 on 10:00 (9:19), 6 x 50 on :45 (:27)

6 x 50 on :45 (:27), 300 on 3:15 (2:47), 6 x 50 on :45 (:27), 600 on 6:30 (5:34), 6 x 50 on :45 (:27), 900 on 9:45 (8:21), 6 x 50 on :45 (:27), 300 FAST (2:38)

## January

8 x (200 on 3:00 (1:46), 100 on 2:00 (:51))

5 x 1000 on 10:00 (9:41, 9:34, 9:32, 9:31, 9:29)

20 x 50 on :30 (:26), 200 ez, 16 x 50 on :35 (:25), 200 ez, 12 x 50 on :40 (:24), 8 x 50 on :45 (:23), 200 ez, 4 x 50 on :50 (22.9, 22.8, 22.7, 22.6)

3 x 1500 on 16:30   (500 ez, 500 moderate, 500 fast)  14:47, (750 moderate, 750 fast) 14:34, 1500 fast 13:57

6 x 1000 descend 1 – 3, 4 – 6 (# 6 faster than # 3)
2 x (10:30, 10:00, 9:30) went 10:04, 9:45, 9:28, then 10:04, 9:48, 9:19

100 free 1:00, 100 fly 1:00, 50 ez on 1:00, 100 free 1:00, 2 x 50 fly :35, 50 ez on 1:00, 100 free on 1:00, 4 x 25 fly on :25, 50 ez on 1:00, 100 free on 1:00, 100 fly on 1:00, 50 ez on 1:00, 100 free on 1:00, 2 x 50 fly on :35, 300 ez then went:

5 x (100 free on 1:00, 100 back on 1:00, 50 ez on 1:00)
15 x 200 on 2:30 for best average wearing a body suit: averaged 1:44.6 # 1 – 13, went 1:43.7 on # 14, 1:42.5 on # 15
800 free pull on 9:00 (7:59), 5 x 100 free on 1:20 (500 pace + :02 + :52), 600 free pull on 7:00 (5:59), 5 x 100 on 1:30 (500 pace = :50), 400 free pull on 5:00 (3:59), 4 x 50 ib :50 (200 pace = :23), 200 free pull on 3:00 (1:59), 4 x 50 free on 1:00 (averaged :22.3)
3 x 1650 free on 17:30  2 x recovery (16:29, 16:30) then 1 x fast 15:15

     Chuck Warner

<u>**February**</u>

500 on 5:30 (4:47), 5 x 100 on 1:00 (:54), :30 rest, 500 on 5:30 (4:37), 10 x 50 on :30 (:26), :30 rest, 500 on 5:30 (4:34), 20 x 25 on :15 (:12.8), :30 rest, 500 fast (4:27)

3 x 400 IM on 5:15 descend 1 – 3 (4:17, 4:10, 4:06) sent him to put on body suit, he came back and went 3:49 on all of these 1, 2 & 4 strong, 3 & 5 fast:

5 x 100 on 1:00 (:55, :55, :51, :53, :50), 5 x 200 on 2:00 (1:54, 1:53, 1:46, 1:54, 1:45), 5 x 400 on 4:00 (3:49, 3:48, 3:36, 3:49, 3:36), 5 x 200 on 2:00 (1:54, 1:54, 1:47, 1:53, 1;45), 5 x 100 on 1:00 (:54, :54, :51, :56 50.0)

Three days before Conference: 15 x 100 on 1:00 (averaged :52.6 for first 14 and went :51.3 on last one)

<u>**March**</u>

200 on 2:30 at 1:55, (1:55), 400 on 4:30 at 3:45 (3:45), 600 on 6:30 at 5:35 (5:34), 800 on 8:30 at 7:25 (7:24), 1000 on 10:30 at 9:15 (9:08)

5 x 100 on 1:00 (:53), :30 rest, 4 x 100 on :58 (:53), :30 rest, 3 x 100 free on :56 (:51.8), :30 rest, 2 x 100 free on :54 (:51+), :30 rest, 1 x 100 on :52 (48.2)

*Careers are ever changing. The partial list of UT swimming and diving grads below is only meant as a depiction of the success so many of these alums have had in their careers.*

**Brad Aiken '00** — Trial lawyer (Edison, McDowell, Hetherington), Houston, TX

**Chris Archer '97** — Professional photographer, Austin, TX

**Carlos Arena '98** — Director of Bitcoin Startup, former VP Goldman Sachs, former director Deutsche, NYC

**Ricky Berens '10** — Nulo Food sales, Austin, TX

**Ross Binkley '03** — goTransverse director of implementation, with National Instruments prior to that, Austin, TX

**Robert Bogart '02** — Apple software engineer, San Francisco, CA

**James Bonney '93** — Senior developer, Broomfire, Austin, TX

**Ken Bostock '85** — VP Customer Service, Hertz, formerly same with United Airlines, Chicago, IL

**Clay Britt '83** — First VP, Morgan Stanley Wealth Management, Bethesda, MD

**Craig Brockman '97** — Founding partner, Viceroy Commercial Realty, Austin, TX

**Nathan Breazeale '87** — Orthopedic surgeon, Austin, TX

**Patrick Brundage '89** — Principal, Axtria Insights (analytics), Scottsdale, AZ

**Russell Chozick '00** — VP, Flashback Data (data recovery), Austin, TX

**Brian Cisna '89** — Mortgage lender, Capital One, Austin, TX

**Bryan Collins '10** — Associate at Kayne Anderson Energy Funds, Houston, TX

**Blake Copple '07** — Navy SEAL, San Diego, CA

**Chris Cornman '91** — Dentist, Georgetown, TX

**Todd Crosset '82** — PhD, Professor of Sport Mgmt, UMass-Amherst, Amherst, MA

**Ian Crocker '04** — Swim clinician & coach, Austin, TX

**Jack Currin, '90** — PhD, Psychologist, pain rehab, rehab med, Tyler, TX

**Doug Dickinson '92** — Morgan Stanley adviser, Milwaukee, WI

**Josh Davis '94**— Business owner, Head Coach Oklahoma Christian College, Oklahoma City, OK

**Kent Dickson '88** — Orthopedic Surgeon, Flower Mound, TX

**Dru Dunworth '83** — Owner, OSS Medical Sales, Austin, TX

**Andre Duplessis '90** — COO, Presbyterian/St. Luke's Children's Hospital, Denver, CO

**Nate Dusing '01** — Orthopedic sales, Austin, TX

**Andy Eckerman '99** — VP Digital Technology, Clayton Homes, Knoxville, TN

**Chris Eckerman '97** — State of Wisconsin Investment Board, Madison, WI

**Doug Elenz '85** — Orthopedic surgeon, Austin, TX

**Rip Esselstyn '87** — Food writer (NY Times Best Seller), with products sold worldwide at Whole Foods, Austin, TX

**Brian Esway '99** — Financial adviser, Eagle Strategies, Austin, TX

**Tomer Feingold '03** — Creative marketing strategies (search engine optimization), former Director World Markets for Oppenheimer, China or Israel

**Ric Fields '84** — Renowned landscape architect, Fieldscape, Vail/Beaver Creek, CO

**Eric Finical '83** — Radiologist, Greenville, NC

**Ken Flaherty '86** — Stryker Orthopaedics sales, Austin, TX

**Sean Foley '03** — Sports media exec, 31 media ventures, in charge of Team Roma soccer business operations and marketing, Austin and NYC

**Colin Gaffney '05** — Assoc attorney, Jorgeson Pittman, Austin, TX

**Scott Goldblatt '01** — Aha! Labs product management, Kansas City, KS

**Tom Hannan '02** — Business consultant, Austin, TX

**Brendan Hansen '04** — Swim coach, business owner, Austin, TX

**John Henry '81** — Roofing company owner, Austin, TX

**Brad Hibbard '91** — Director, Healthier Populations, Orion Health, Orange County, CA

**Whitney Hite '96** — Assistant swimming coach, Univ of Arizona, Tucson, AZ

**Martin Hubbell '96** — Atty, Diehl & Hubbell, LLC, Lebanon, OH

**Scott Hunt '01** — Principal broker, Equus Realty, Louisville, KY

**Lee Jamieson '87** — Owner, Pacifico Energy , Bakersfield, CA

**Jonathan Jennings '94** — Executive sales, PDX Software, Dallas, TX

**Bryan Jones '00** — Entrepreneur, Austin, TX

**Robert N. Jones '87** — Securities litigation consultant, Charlottesville, VA

**Shaun Jordan '91** — Securities trading, Austin, TX

**David Kahn '06** — Dentist, Miller Place, NY

**Paul Kaump '00 (transferred)** — President, Biz Plan Reviews (oversees over $800 million in assets), Minneapolis, MN

**John Kenny '82** — Owner, Sierra Properties (commercial real estate), Dallas, TX

**Ramon Kik '98** — Project engineer, Lockheed Martin, Houston, TX

**Bob Kitzman '87** — Sr VP at US Trust, DFW, TX

**Paul Latimer '98** — PhD, Sr Medical Liaison Genentech, Austin, TX

**John Littlepage '09** — Reservoir engineer, BP Petroleum, Trinidad

**Joe Lajoie '82** — Race engineer, Vehicle Dynamics Performance (Indy race cars), Austin, TX

**Agustin Magruder '09** — Production engineer, Pioneer Natural Resources ,Dallas, TX

**Spencer Martin '88** — PhD, Professor of finance, Univ of Melbourne, Melbourne, Australia

**Steve Martyak '98** — High tech, Austin, TX

**Austin McAnally '04** — President, SuiteRx, Austin, TX

**David McClellan '89** — Forum Financial adviser, Chicago, IL

**Matt McGinnis '11** — Tech writer for bioMerieux, Raleigh, NC

**Sean McGrath '99** — President, Capital Wealth Management, Newport Beach, CA

**Matt Molnar '06** — Project Engineer, L3 Communications, Waco, TX

**Colin Murtagh '09** — Associate brand strategist, Twitter, Los Angeles, CA

**Philip Nenon '82** — Director, adviser, Crimson Medical, Tucson, AZ

**Nick Nevid '03** — PhD, Consultant, Aquaculture Industry, Dallas, TX

**Greg Norman '03** — Dell until 2015, now Spectranetics, Dallas, TX

**William Paulus '83** — Orthodontist, Ft Worth, TX

**Aaron Peirsol '04** — Carpenter, International Swimming Hall of Fame Executive Board, Newport Beach, CA

**Poston Pritchitt '07** — Attorney, Andrews Meyers, Houston, TX

**Joe Poe '82** — Consultant, ACAP Securities, Oklahoma City, OK

**Ken Quarterman '88** — Eclipse Defense Strategies sales, Captain of commercial fishing ship, Boise, ID

**Mark Ragusa '87** — Business litigation attorney, Tampa, FL

**Andy Rasmussen '87** — Merrill Lynch Wealth Mgmt, Austin, TX

**Jamie Rauch '01** — Retired portfolio manager with Chicago Board of Trade, Chicago, IL

**Kelly Rives '82** — Project manager, Oceaneering Oil Fields, Houston, TX

**CJ Robie '97** — Strategic Account Manager, Adobe, San Diego, CA

**Dan Rohleder '08** — Contract attorney for Accenture, Atlanta, GA

**Bill Robertson '81** — Owner, Camp Longhorn, Burnet, TX

**Kenneth Eric Ruby '90** — Urologist, Somerset, KY

**Wyatt Russo '96** — Sr VP, The Retail Connection (commercial realty), Dallas, TX

**Kyle Sanders '02** — Sr Mgr Brand Development, Academy Sports, Houston, TX

WE COULD NOT HAVE REACHED THE DEPTH THAT WE DID in this book without the help of many people. The willingness of Elinor Reese, Holly Reese Bowman and Heather Reese Ormond to pull back the curtain of their family's life has been essential. Kris Kubik's service to the research and accuracy of this book pales in comparison to what he has given to Texas swimmers but was nonetheless boundless in its contribution. Bill Robertson's communication with the Working Exes for Texas Swimming (WETS) helped us find many alums. The speed with which Longhorn swimmers and coaching colleagues jumped to help us was an inspiration and invigorating. Their stories are the heart of this book.

Credits for each photo are in the back of the book. The brilliance of the photographers shines through these pages. The talent and generosity of Peter Bick and Taylor Brien of Swimming World Magazine, Andy Ringgold (father of UT great Brett Ringgold) and a small army of people in the Texas Athletic Department led by Jill Sterkel and Jim Sigmon brought great life to this story. The personal memorabilia and archives of swim stars Nick Nevid and William Paulus provided a great glimpse into the history of the early Reese years. Retired UT sports information chief Bill Little provided valuable guidance. A special thanks to Olympian Kathleen Hersey, who was one of the rare women coached regularly by Eddie Reese, for capturing a poignant moment with her camera in chapter 5, page 55.

Fortunately, the sport of swimming and Coach Reese's career has been widely reported on. The availability of the records of *Swimming World Magazine*, the American Swimming Coaches Association and SwimSwam.com were indispensable in the development of this book.

Our production required endless edits from the artistic eyes and minds of Todd Kemmerling and Jeri Leer, as well as editorial guidance and suggestions from Sandra Bledsoe Landtroop. The early readers, Scott Hammond, Terry Warner, Casey Converse and Bob Carbone provided helpful advice. Patricia Marshall's staff at Luminare Press gave a little extra drop of love to their work for Eddie and Elinor, and for that we will always be especially grateful.

Finally, thank you to Mr. DeLoss Dodds for your support. It meant a great deal to us nearly forty years ago, just as it did in completing this work.

# FOOTNOTES

*Prologue*

1. "It's good to…" MTMP (Many Times, Many Places; often used)

*Chapter 1 "Mom Always Liked Me Best"*

1. "I'll retire when…" – Chris O'Connell, "Stroke of Genius: How Eddie Reese Turned Texas Men's Swimming and Diving into the Best Program in the Nation," *The Alcalde* (Alumni Magazine of The University of Texas), January 1, 2018

2. "I took three…" – American Swimming Coaches Association (ASCA), "Interview With Olympic Head Swim Coaches Eddie Reese and Jack Bauerle, by Mark Schubert," 2007 World Clinic Yearbook

3. "If a bomb…" – Dana Abbott, personal recollection, 2009

4. "You've heard of…" – Kris Kubik, personal recollection, interview with Dana Abbott, May 2018

5. "Do three and…" – Dana Abbott, personal recollection; also MTMP

6. "Swimming is too…" – Swimmingworldmagazine.com, Video Interview: "Eddie Reese and Will Licon on Longhorns' Team Championship," March 26, 2016

7. "Come back when…" – MTMP

8. "The key is…" – "Eddie Reese", texassports.com

*Chapter 2 "Competitiveness"*

1. "I like to…" – John Smith '84, personal recollection (chapter heading; repeated in text)

2. "If everyone on…" – "Texas Swimming and Diving Big 12 Championships Preview" (Video), texassports.com

3. "We have a…" – "Texas Swimming and Diving Big 12 Championships Preview" (Video), ibid.

4. "When I go…" – Mark Muckenfuss, "Close To Perfect",
   *Swimming World Magazine,* May 1990, p. 35

5. "You don't sleep…" – Bob Ingram, "TEAM TEXAS", *Swimming
   World Magazine,* May 1991, p. 80

6. "The rewards have…" – "Texas Swimming and Diving Big 12
   Championships Preview" (Video), ibid.

7. "Personally, I try…" – ibid.

8. "Now when we…" – Bob Schaller, "20 Question Tuesday: Eddie
   Reese," USA Swimming, January 2, 2018

### Chapter 3 "Recruiting"

1. "All I recruit…" – ASCA, "What To Do And How To Do It",
   1997 World Clinic Yearbook.

2. "There are plenty…" – Chuck Warner, personal recollection

3. "I'd rather be…" – MTMP; also Chase Kreitler, personal journal

4. "The best people…" – MTMP

5. "The best recruiting…" – O'Connell (paraphrased), op. cit.

### Chapter 4 "Coaching College Men"

1. "I've coached eighteen…" – MTMP

2. "Even though I…" – http://thinkexist.com/quotes/eddie_reese/

3. "Teaching physical education…" – (Video), "40 on the Forty –
   Eddie Reese Relives His Four-Decade Dynasty," texassports.
   com, March 29, 2018

4. "Better to be…" – Aaron Peirsol, personal recollection, via email
   to Chuck Warner, November 2017

5. "Why don't you…" – Kubik, op. cit.

6. "It was important…" – Katie Arris-Wilson, personal
   recollection, via email

7. "All over the…" – Kreitler, op. cit.

8. "Swimming has the…" – Dana Abbott, personal recollection;
   also MTMP

9. "The only people…" – Phone conversation with Chuck Warner,
   1981

*Chapter 5 "Eddie's Coach"*

1.  "There are three…" – ASCA, "Interview With Eddie Reese by Chuck Warner," 2006 World Clinic Yearbook

2.  "Mom was on…" – ibid.

3.  "She could beat…" – ibid.

4.  "Roses are red…" – Elinor Reese, joint interview with Chuck Warner and Dana Abbott, March 2018

5.  "They were great…" – ibid.

6.  "The key is …" – Personal conversation with Chuck Warner, 2016

7.  "The tougher the…" – Phone conversation with Chuck Warner, July 2018

8.  "I wouldn't have…" – ibid.

*Chapter 6 "Leadership"*

1.  "Bear the pain" – MTMP; also ASCA, "Motivation – How To Get Them To Do More Than They Want," 2001 World Clinic Yearbook; ASCA, "Strength: How to Get Stronger in Each Level," 2009 World Clinic Yearbook; Avrel Seale, "Coach Reese's Ultimate Challenge," *The Alcalde,* July/August 2001

2.  "The main thing…" – Quoting Stephen Covey, "The 7 Habits of Highly Effective People," Free Press, 1989

3.  "Have patience or…" – "The Past, Present, and Future of Swimming," interview moderated by Chuck Warner, *American Swimming Magazine,* Volume 2018, Edition 1, p. 16

*Chapter 7 "Motivation"*

1.  "I don't yell…" – "The Past, Present, and Future of Swimming," op. cit., p. 17

2.  "Take it upon…" – Kreitler, op. cit.

3.  "One of the…" – "Men's Swimming and Diving 101," texassports. com, October 6, 2004

4.  "I tried to…" – MTMP

5.  "As hard as…" – Coleman Hodges, "What Makes Eddie Reese Great?" (Video), swimswam.com, Nov 9, 2017

6. "If you want ..." – Kreitler, op. cit.

7. "I see them..." – ASCA, "Motivation: How To Get Them To Do More Than They Want", 2001 World Clinic Yearbook

8. "When you get..." – Personal conversation with Chuck Warner during research for *... And Then They Won Gold,* 2012

9. "This sport chooses..." – Lydia Chase, via email, personal recollection from 1990 training trip to U.S. Olympic Training Center; also MTMP

## *Chapter 8 "Strength"*

1. "If I can..." – ASCA, 1977 World Clinic Yearbook

2. "My guys have..." – ibid.

3. "You can hold..." – MTMP

4. "In a vertical..." – Dana Abbott, personal recollection from UT practice, 1978

5. "Was he flexing?" – "Eddie Reese, Texas," video interview, Swimming World YouTube Channel, March 23, 2017

6. "I unlock the..." – Dana Abbott, personal recollection in answer to question, "How do you motivate them in the weight room?" asked at ASCA World Clinic

7. "If somebody has..." – ASCA, "Strength: How To Get Stronger in Each Level," op. cit.

## *Chapter 9 "Technique"*

1. "Stroke work is..." – "The Past, Present, and Future of Swimming," op. cit., p. 16

2. "You've got to..." – "Eddie Reese on Swimming" (DVD), Championship Productions, Ames IA

3. "Don't put a..." – Chuck Warner, personal recollection

4. "There are no..." – Dana Abbott, personal recollection from UT practice, 1978

5. "This meet (NCAAs) is..." – "Attention to Detail in Season Helping Texas at NCAAs," Video, swimmingworldmagazine.com, March 26, 2015

6. "Going faster isn't..." – "Eddie Reese on Swimming" (DVD), op. cit.

7. "Coaches can't make…" – Kreitler, op. cit.; also MTMP

8. "The best entry…" – "The Past, Present, and Future of Swimming," op.cit., p. 15

9. "If straight arm…" – Chuck Warner, personal recollection

10. "The longer the…" – "The Past, Present, and Future of Swimming", op.cit., p. 15

11. "The best kickers…" – ibid.

12. "Other strokes have…" – "Eddie Reese on Swimming" (DVD), op. cit.

13. "The strongest and…" – "The Past, Present, and Future of Swimming", op.cit., p. 15

14. "The finish of…" – ibid.

15. "In breaststroke, you…" – MTMP

16. "It's the hardest…" – "Eddie Reese on Swimming" (DVD), op. cit.

17. "When your arms…" – "The Past, Present, and Future of Swimming" (paraphrased), op. cit., p. 16

18. "It's a very…" – "Eddie Reese on Swimming" (DVD), op. cit.

19. "If you can't…" – Braden Keith, "Texas Coach Eddie Reese Reveals Secret to Butterfly Dynasty," SwimSwam.com, March 3, 2015

20. "The best way…" – "The Past, Present, and Future of Swimming", op.cit., p. 15

21. "If you feel …" – "Eddie Reese on Swimming" (DVD), op. cit.

22. "When they flashed…" – "Eddie Reese's Heart Rate 'Got Above 50' after 100 Fly Prelims" (Video), swimmingworldmagazine.com, March 27, 2015


*Chapter 10 "Kris Kubik"*

1. "Kris is a…" – Schaller, ibid.

2. "Every once in…" – "Kris Kubik Announces Retirement after 34 Seasons at Texas," texassports.com, July 18, 2016

3. "He makes sure…" – Travis Feldhaus, "Longhorn Hall of Honor: Kris Kubik," Texas Media Relations, texassports.com, November 19, 2011

4. "He's just a…" – -ibid.

5. "We were lucky…" – Schaller, ibid.

6. "There is no…" – "Kris Kubik announces retirement after 34 seasons at Texas," op. cit.

7. "Caring. Genius. Best. …" – Courtesy Bill Robertson, Working Exes for Texas Swimming (WETS),


**Chapter 11 "Training"**

1. "If it was…" – MTMP

2. "This sport is…" – Kreitler, op. cit.

3. "We had a…" – Coleman Hodges, "Eddie Reese Video Interview: Jack/Joe Showdown Pt. 2" (Video), swimswam.com, March 27, 2015

4. "There is a…" – Chuck Warner, "Eddie Reese: A Coach's Life," *American Swimming Magazine,* Volume 2017, Issue 2, p. 9

5. "If you're not…" – Coleman Hodges, "Eddie Reese Shares Winter Training Workouts" (Video), swimswam.com, January 18, 2018

6. "Socktember… Rocktober… Slowvember…" – Coleman Hodges, "What Makes Eddie Reese Great?" (Video), swimswam.com, Nov 9, 2017

7. "Once you get …" – Michael J. Stott, "Lessons With The Legends: Eddie Reese," *Swimming World,* March 2016, p. 10

8. "If you use…" – David Rieder, "EDDIE REESE: All about Swimming with the Legendary Texas Coach," *Swimming Technique,* November 2017, p. 22

9. "If you swim…" – Ronnie Paul, personal recollection, ca. 1979

10. "You have to…" – Stott, op. cit.

11. "All swim meets…" (paraphrased) – S/W, "Eddie Reese, Joseph Schooling, and Kip Darmody, Texas (after night 3)" (Video), March 28, 2015

12. "At the end…" – Stott, op. cit.

*Chapter 12 "Taper"*

1. "Taper is an…" (paraphrased) – C. Hodges, "Eddie Reese – Taper Is an Art No One Understands" (Video), swimswam.com, June 7, 2016.

2. "Taper is determined…" – ASCA, "Strength: How to Get Stronger in Each Level," op. cit.

3. "I know for…" – ASCA, "Senior Training," 2005 World Clinic Yearbook

4. "You can't rest…" – Dana Abbott, personal recollection, 1979

5. "If they don't…" – ASCA, "Strength: How To Get Stronger in Each Level," op. cit.

6. "Racing freestyle takes…" – ASCA, "Senior Training," op. cit.

7. "I do have…" – ASCA, "Strength: How To Get Stronger in Each Level," op. cit.

8. "Sometimes you just…" – Chuck Warner, "Eddie Reese: A Coach's Life," *American Swimming Magazine,* Volume 2017, Issue 2, p. 9


*Chapter 13 "Winning"*

1. "I can't tell…" – Maria Cowley, Keshav Prathivadi, "Longhorns Become Winningest Program in History with 13th National Title," *Daily Texan,* March 26, 2017

2. "Eighty percent like…" – Wills Layton, "Reese Brings Championship Experience in 39th Season," *Daily Texan,* November 2, 2016

3. "That's why he's…" – Chuck Warner, personal conversation

4. "Somebody wished me…" – Mark Muckenfuss, "Texas Does It Back-To-Back," *Swimming World,* May 1989, p. 31

5. "At my age…" – Bob Ingram, "Focus and Finish," *Swimming World,* May 1996, p. 29

6. "Our philosophy has…"- Kari Lyderson, "Texas Turnaround," *Swimming World,* May 2005, p. 22

7. "This [last night 2010]…" – "Texas Captures 10th NCAA Men's Swimming and Diving Championship," texassports.com, March 28, 2010

8. "I don't know…" – Layton, op. cit.

9. "As good as…" – Conference with UT swimmer (names and dates withheld for privacy)

10. "I need you…" – ibid.

11. "If you should…" – ibid.

12. "There is something…" – ibid.

13. "I really appreciate…" – ibid.

14. "We generally know…" – ibid.

15. "You have so…" – ibid.

16. "To do something…" – ibid.

17. " Don't do it…" – Kris Kubik, op. cit.

18. "Take care of…" – O'Connell, op. cit.; also MTMP

### Chapter 14 *"A Living Legacy"*

1. "We have a…" – "Texas Swimming and Diving Big 12 Championships Preview" (Video), ibid.

2. "We know swimming…" – "Men's Swimming and Diving 101," texassports.com, October 6, 2004

3. "When you have…" – Speech at 2016 team banquet

### Chapter 15 *"Around The Corner"*

1. "I think I'm…" – O'Connell, op. cit

2. "I'm fixed…" – "Texas Coach Eddie Reese on the Mend after Heart Surgery," swimswam.com, January 26, 2011

3. "If I didn't…" – Stott, op. cit.

4. "I like being…" – "Men's Swimming and Diving 101," op.cit

5. "I've either been…" – David Rieder, "Eddie Reese – All About Swimming with the Legendary Texas Coach," *Swimming Technique Magazine,* Oct/Nov/Dec 2017; also MTMP

6. "You can't make…" – ASCA, World Clinic Interview, 2017

7. "I'm going to…" – Chuck Warner, personal conversation, 2017.

8. "If I can't…" – Dana Abbott, personal recollection, TISCA high school coaches clinic, early 1980s

9.  "I've been to…" – "The Past, Present, and Future of Swimming,"
    op.cit., p. 12

10. "When I go…" – ibid.

11. "I paid to…" – ibid.

12. "When you die…" – Schaller, ibid.

                    Chuck Warner

# PHOTOGRAPHY SOURCES

**Peter Bick**

| | |
|---|---|
| *Chapter 2* | *Townley Haas* |
| *Chapter 3* | *Texas Swim Center* |
| *Chapter 4* | *Coaching College Men* |
| *Chapter 6* | *Eddie with McBroom* |
| *Chapter 7* | *1:29.5 Scoreboard* |
| | *Aaron Peirsol* |
| | *Josh Davis* |
| *Chapter 9* | *Muscle Rolling* |
| | *Shebat Start* |
| | *100 Fly Board* |
| *Chapter 10* | *Kris & Eddie* |
| | *Kris w/towel* |
| *Chapter 12* | *Taper, Walk on Water* |
| | *Ian Crocker* |
| *Chapter 13* | *Neil Walker* |
| | *Divers* |
| | *Hug* |
| *Chapter 14* | *Handshake* |
| *Chapter 15* | *Joseph Schooling* |
| | *Reese & Bauerle* |
| | *Eddie, When you die* |

**Taylor Brien**

*Cover photo*

**Courtesy Cactus Yearbook, University of Texas at Austin**

*Chapter 2*  *Eddie's Inaugural Squad*

*Chapter 2*　　　　UF Captains
*Chapter 3*　　　　Mom Always Liked Me Best
*Chapter 5*　　　　Elinor's 21st birthday
　　　　　　　　　Wedding Day

## Bill Robertson

*Chapter 1*　　　　Mike Brown
*Chapter 3*　　　　Eddie & Coach Patterson
　　　　　　　　　Eddie & Richard Quick
*Chapter 13*　　　1981 Team
*Chapter 15*　　　SHHH

## Texas Sports

*Chapter 1*　　　　Eddie brings a smile
*Chapter 2*　　　　Competitiveness
　　　　　　　　　Eddie yelling
　　　　　　　　　Doug Gjertsen
*Chapter 3*　　　　Recruiting, Eddie & Kris
　　　　　　　　　Shaun Jordan
*Chapter 5*　　　　Swim Camp
*Chapter 7*　　　　Motivation. Yell FOR Them
*Chapter 8*　　　　Eddie Strength
*Chapter 9*　　　　Eddie Tech
*Chapter 10*　　　Kris & Eddie 1987
*Chapter 11*　　　Eddie with Gjerstsen & Werth

## Texas Swimming & Diving Hall of Fame

*Chapter 6*　　　　Coach McMillion

## Annie Warner

*Author's Photo*

CHUCK WARNER has served as a USA National Team Coach three-times, coached three NCAA DII runners-up teams and seven National Y Championship teams. Coach Warner has served two terms as President of the American Swimming Coaches Association and on the Board of Directors for the International Swimming Hall of Fame. Warner has previously authored two highly acclaimed books (*Four Champions, One Gold Medal & …And Then They Won Gold*) as well as numerous articles for *Swimming World* and the *ASCA Magazines,* as well as *SwimSwam.com.* Chuck and Dana Abbott were assistant coaches on Eddie Reese's first staff at Texas and have collaborated previously on books and articles.

DANA ABBOTT swam at Tulane University and coached in Mississippi and Alabama before starting grad school at Texas. After working 1978-80 with Eddie Reese, was head coach at Katy (TX) High School for 25 years, and 12 more years in Katy at St. John XXIII. He has been a speaker/clinician locally, nationally, and internationally, president of TISCA and twice president of NISCA. Has previously worked with Chuck Warner on *And Then They Won Gold* and several articles in *Swimming World Magazine.*